Environmentalism

Short Histories of Big Ideas Series List

Published   *Capitalism* By Paul Bowles

Feminism By June Hannam

Environmentalism By David Peterson del Mar

Communism By Mark Sandle

Available soon   *Fascism* By Martin Blinkhorn

Nationalism By Richard Bosworth

Zionism By David Engel

Terrorism By Rosemary O'Kane

Modernism By Robin Walz

Environmentalism

DAVID PETERSON DEL MAR

Harlow, England • London • New York • Boston • San Francisco • Toronto
Sydney • Tokyo • Singapore • Hong Kong • Seoul • Taipei • New Delhi
Cape Town • Madrid • Mexico City • Amsterdam • Munich • Paris • Milan

PEARSON EDUCATION LIMITED

Edinburgh Gate
Harlow CM20 2JE
United Kingdom
Tel: +44 (0)1279 623623
Fax: +44 (0)1279 431059
Website: www.pearsoned.co.uk

First edition published in Great Britain in 2006

ISBN-13: 978-0-582-77297-7
ISBN-10: 0-582-77297-4

British Library Cataloguing in Publication Data
A CIP catalogue record for this book can be obtained from the British Library

Library of Congress Cataloging in Publication Data
A CIP catalog record for this book can be obtained from the Library of Congress

10   9   8   7   6   5   4   3   2   1
10   09   08   07   06

Set by 35 in 9/15pt Iowan
Printed and Bound in Malaysia

The Publisher's policy is to use paper manufactured from sustainable forests.

For my students

Contents

Series Editor's Preface

WHAT MAKES THE WORLD MOVE? Great men? Irresistible forces? Catastrophic events?

When listening to the morning news on the radio, reading our daily newspapers, following debates on the internet, watching evening television, all of these possibilities – and more – are offered as explanations of the troubles that beset the world in the Middle East, the 'war on terror' in Iraq and Afghanistan, environmental disasters at Chernobyl or New Orleans, and genocide in Sudan or Rwanda.

Where should we look to find answers to the puzzles of the present? To psychology? To economics? To sociology? To political science? To philosophy? Each of these disciplines offer insights into the personalities and the subterranean forces that propel the events that change the world, and within each of these disciplines there are experts who dissect current affairs on the foundation of these insights.

But all of these events, these problems, and even these disciplines themselves have one thing in common: they have a history. And it is through an understanding of the history of those ideas that inspired the people behind the events, and the ideas behind the ideologies that attempted to explain and control the forces around them that we can comprehend the perplexing and confusing world of the present day.

'Short Histories of Big Ideas' aims to provide readers with clear, concise and readable explanations of those ideas that were instrumental in shaping the twentieth century and that continue to shape – and reshape – the present. Everyone who attempts to follow the events of today via newspapers, television, radio and the internet cannot help but see or hear references to 'capitalism', 'communism', 'feminism', 'environmentalism', 'nationalism', 'colonialism' and many other 'isms'. And, while most of us probably believe that we have a basic understanding of what these terms mean, we are probably much less certain about who it was that coined, invented or defined them. Even more murky is our understanding of how these concepts moved from an idea to become an ideology and, perhaps, a phenomenon that changed the world. Most bewildering may be the disputes and controversies between factions and divisions within the movements and political parties that claim to be the true followers and the legitimate heirs of those who first conceived of the concepts to which they claim to adhere.

The authors of these Short Histories have been asked to write accessible, jargon-free prose with the goal of making comprehensible to the intelligent, interested but non-expert reader these highly complicated concepts. In each instance the approach taken is chronological, as each author attempts to explain the origins of these ideas, to describe the people who created them and then to follow the twisting path they followed from conception to the present. Each author in the series is an expert in the field, with a mastery of the literature on the subject – and a desire to convey to readers the knowledge and the understanding that the research of specialist scholars has produced, but which is normally inaccessible to those not engaged in studying these subjects in an academic environment.

The work of specialists often seems remote, obscure, even pedantic, to the non-specialist, but the authors in this series are committed to the goal of bringing the insights and understanding of specialists to a wider public, to concerned citizens and general readers who wish to go beyond today's headlines and form a more comprehensive and meaningful picture of today's world.

Gordon Martel

Timeline

1907   Boy Scouts founded in England

1914   France's first national park

1917   Spain's first national park

1920   First national park in the Soviet Union

1934   Germany becomes the first nation to protect wolves

1942   Disney's *Bambi*

1949   Aldo Leopold, *A Sand County Almanac*

1952   London Smog

1956   Dam on Colorado River blocked in US

1963   Rachel Carson's *Silent Spring*
       Partial Test Ban Treaty

1964   Wilderness Act in US

1968   Edward Abbey's *Desert Solitaire*
       Paul Ehrlich, *The Population Bomb*
       The Undersea World of Jacques Cousteau premieres
       Sweden's Environmental Protection Law

1969   *Torrey Canyon* oil spill
       Radical student protests in western Europe
       Friends of the Earth founded in the US

1970   Earth Day

1971   Greenpeace founded in Canada

1972   Club of Rome, *Limits to Growth*
       Arne Naess coins the term 'Deep Ecology'
       West Germany's Council of Environmental Experts established
       United Nations Stockholm Conference on the Human Environment

1973   British Royal Commission on Environmental Pollution established
       Peter Singer coins the term 'animal liberation'

1975   Great Barrier Reef Marine Park founded

1978   Toxic wastes found at Love Canal in US

1980   Earth First! founded in US
       People for the Ethical Treatment of Animals founded
       in US

1983   West Germany's Green Party wins representation in the
       Bündestag

1986   Accident at Chernobyl nuclear power plant in the Soviet
       Union

1987   World Commission on the Environment stresses sustain-
       able development

1989   The Green Parties of the United Kingdom and France win
       10 and 15 per cent of the vote, respectively, in national
       elections

1991   Founding of the People of Color Environmental Leadership
       in the US

1992   United Nations Rio de Janeiro Summit

1998   Keiko returns to Iceland

Who's Who for *Environmentalism*

Edward Abbey, 1927–1989. U.S. novelist and essayist, radical environmentalist.

David Brower, 1912–2000. U.S. environmentalist, founder of Friends of the Earth.

Sally Carrighar, 1898–1985. U.S. author of nature books.

Rachel Carson, 1907–1964. Popular U.S. biologist, author of *Silent Spring*.

Jacques Cousteau, 1910–1997. Popular French oceanographer.

John Denver, 1943–1997. Popular U.S. singer who celebrated wild places.

Petra Kelly, 1947–1992. West German Green Party leader.

Aldo Leopold, 1887–1948. U.S. ecologist, author of *A Sand County Almanac*.

George Perkins Marsh, 1801–1882. U.S. conservationist, author of *Man and Nature*.

David McTaggart, 1932–2001. Canadian environmentalist, long-time Greenpeace leader.

Farley Mowat, 1921–. Canadian author of many nature books.

John Muir, 1838–1914. U.S. wilderness advocate, writer, president of the Sierra Club.

Arne Naess, 1912–. Norwegian philosopher, founder of Deep Ecology.

Beatrix Potter, 1866–1943. British author of children's books featuring animals.

Robert Redford, 1936–. U.S. actor, entrepreneur, outdoor enthusiast.

Jean-Jacques Rousseau, 1712–1778. French writer and philosopher, celebrant of nature.

E. F. Schumacher, 1911–1977. British economist, author of *Small is Beautiful*.

Gary Snyder, 1930–. U.S. poet, radical environmentalist.

Henry David Thoreau, 1817–1862. U.S. transcendentalist, nature advocate, author of *Walden*.

William Wordsworth, 1770–1850. British poet and champion of hiking, nature loving.

Acknowledgements

I am grateful to Gordon Martel for both inviting me to write this book and insisting that I do so boldly. He also straightened many kinks in my prose and reasoning.

This book depends on the work of many researchers and writers. I am particularly indebted to Michael Bess, Jon Katz, Roderick Frazier Nash, Jennifer Price, Harriet Ritvo, Keith Thomas, and Meredith Veldman for their diligence and incisiveness.

As always, Wendy del Mar has been a wonderfully warm and supportive life partner who gave the manuscript a very close and critical reading. Paul Semonin also encouraged me. Thank you, Peter, my city boy, for giving me hope that we shall make ourselves at home here.

Introduction

'But I don't want comfort.' Aldous Huxley, *Brave New World*

The project seemed reasonable enough. Americans' consumption of energy continued to climb at the dawn of the twenty-first century, and wind offered a relatively 'green' or clean source of electricity. Locating some 170 energy-producing turbines off windy Cape Cod, on the New England coast, would serve area homes and businesses without the pollution attached to oil, natural gas, or coal.

But residents and their sympathizers raised $3 million to oppose the plan, and they did so in the name of nature preservation. 'Our national treasures should be off limits to industrialization,' explained Walter Cronkite, the retired news anchor.[1] The wind generators would not belch smoke, create acid rain, or require extensive mining. But they would mar the horizon, would constitute a pimple on the smooth cheek of sand, sky, and ocean.

Of course Cronkite's ocean-front home consumed a great deal of nature in its construction and maintenance, and the power which ran it had to come from somewhere. But opponents of the project evidently thought that people living inland, where views and property values were more modest, ought to bear the burden of producing energy for those whose capacious living rooms enjoyed better vistas.

The battle over wind-generated power off Cape Cod illustrates this book's salient themes. *Environmentalism* dwells on the paradoxical relationship between prosperity and nature loving. Professions of concern and affection for the environment have been most powerful among the eras, nations, and people that have most successfully subjected and consumed it. This relationship has been, in some respects, logical. Worries over nature's well being should indeed rise as its health is compromised, and environmentalists have succeeded in regulating the exploitation of natural resources, preserving many parks and other areas, rescuing from extinction many animals and plants, and reducing some pollutants.

But nature loving has more often embodied than challenged the western march of material progress and comfort. People who buy the expensive homes on the shores of Cape Cod may consider themselves refugees from industrial capitalism. Yet only the very wealthy can afford the view, a prized window onto a 'natural' world that is every bit as much of a consumer good as the luxury cars in the driveway.

We revere nature not so much because it provides us with food, shelter, and tools, but because it offers meaning. Western peoples have become progressively ignorant of and disinterested in how soil, water, animals, trees, and other plants sustain our bodies, more and more adamant that these things feed our souls, that they transport us to a pure place beyond our superficial, everyday lives.

This book will spend considerable ink on the development of ideas and practices having to do with the conservation and preservation of particular parts of the environment, including some, like forestry, that have been highly technical in nature. But we shall study these political and economic movements in the context of much broader cultural forces, a growing embrace of places, species, and experiences deemed precious and beneficent: nature loving. Unlike programmes of rational conservation, nature loving has been much more concerned with transcending this world, our environment, than with coming to terms with it.

Environmentalism explores the recurring tension between science and emotion, conservation and preservation. The former has taken up the business of establishing a sensible, sustainable way of interacting with nature, which is understood as providing humans with life's necessities, from building materials to clean air. Preservation has been more likely to focus on nature's intangible gifts – the spiritual or national regeneration said to spring from certain places or species.

Class or economic divisions have informed these clashes. Poor people's reliance on plants and animals has often been direct – as has their experience of environmental problems like toxic waste. Well-to-do westerners have been more apt to perceive nature in abstract or symbolic terms and to disguise their reliance on it, like the prosperous Victorians who replaced vegetable with flower gardens, chickens and pigs with pets and cast-iron deer. Ideas about and movements concerned with nature loving have provided venues for people to malign the character of and attack the material interests of people different from themselves.

This book's emphasis on the complexities, divisions, and paradoxes of environmentalism should not be understood as an indictment of environmental movements, a brief for unfettered capitalism. But in exploring the history of nature loving I have become convinced that many of our environmental problems are rooted not simply in the western world's commitment to prosperity and growth but also in environmentalism's tradition of incoherence and irrelevance, its tendency to complement rather than to confront the attitudes and practices behind our growing environmental problems.

I am optimistic and vain enough to hope that *Environmentalism* can play a role in helping a worthy set of impulses and movements become more self-reflective and therefore more relevant and effective.

Note

1   Burkett, E. (2003) 'A Mighty Wind,' *New York Times Magazine*, 15 June, p. 48.

CHAPTER 1

Domesticating
the wild

MEN ON TRAINS WERE NOT supposed to behave this
way. The gentleman was sticking his head out of the window,
exposing himself to the storm. Finally he withdrew, then sat
back, with eyes closed, as if trying to memorize the unpleasant
sensations he had just subjected himself to.

Landscape painter J.M.W. Turner's odd behaviour seemed to
make a mockery of the hard-won comforts of mid-nineteenth-
century England. For millennia travellers had slowly toiled along
at the mercy of the elements. To travel several hundred miles
overland was the work of weeks or months, through all manner
of weather. The railroad had finally changed all of that, had anni-
hilated time and space, cheated sun, wind, cold, and rain. So why
was this Englishman sticking his head into the storm?

Europeans had a long legacy of distrusting and trying to
dominate the environment. Indigenous peoples across the world
emphasized their dependence on a powerful, animate world that
had the power to bestow or withhold sustenance. East Asians,

notwithstanding their technological achievements, perceived nature as a potent force that humans ought to contemplate and learn from. But Christians viewed untamed nature as a threat to their survival, livelihoods, and salvation.

The economic and scientific transformations of the seventeenth and eighteenth centuries made western people less fearful of nature, more confident in their ability to unlock its bounties. Indeed, thoughtful scientists and bureaucrats began to realize that woods and soils were being exploited too successfully, that without programmes of conservation, nations' future prosperity and security would be compromised.

But the emergence of sensible programmes of conservation do not explain the spread of sensibilities such as Turner's, the growing affinity for a nature that seemed appealing precisely because it still lay beyond human control. By the mid-nineteenth century the most prosperous western peoples had turned to nature for instruction and meaning even as they transformed it into a machine that would predictably produce wheat, timber, and other crops.

Christianity dominated medieval Europeans' views of nature. The Judeo-Christian God transcended the earth rather than residing in or emanating from it. Worldly existence was a fleeting prelude to eternal, hopefully heavenly, life.

> *Like the Greeks and Romans before them, medieval Christians asserted that nature made itself available and useful to humans*

Like the Greeks and Romans before them, medieval Christians asserted that nature made itself available and useful to humans. Even Francis of Assisi, a thirteenth-century figure often invoked by modern nature lovers, placed humanity squarely at the head of creation. St. Bonaventure noted approvingly that St. Francis had 'subdued ferocious beasts, tamed the wild, trained the tame and bent to his obedience the brute beasts that had rebelled against fallen mankind' (Coates, 1998, 54). When medieval people expressed appreciation for nature, they had in mind orderly and productive fields, land that they had cleared or drained, and animals that they had domesticated, not the uninhabited places where wild beasts, monsters, and perhaps Satan himself lurked.

Nature's toils and fruits alike could distract good Christians from pursuing a heavenly reward outside this world. Its terrors – drought, wolves, trolls, and worse – could kill, and its pleasures could divert people's attention from God.

Then capitalism emasculated nature. Scientists such as Galileo Galilei, Francis Bacon, René Descartes, and Isaac Newton described nature as passive, a collection of inert materials and mechanistic processes that humans could and should manipulate to further their own ends. Leon Battista Alberti, a fifteenth-century writer, celebrated 'the Rocks cut, Mountains bored through, Vallies filled up, Lakes confined, Marshes discharged into the Sea, Ships built, Rivers turned, their Mouths cleared, Bridges Laid over them, Harbours formed'.[1] Humanity had found the golden key to unlock prosperity's stubborn door. Transportation, commerce, agriculture, and industry accelerated. Yields of wheat and other staples swelled with such inventions and innovations as the seed drill, more efficient ploughs and other implements, and intensified crop rotations – all the fruits of a more experimental, scientific, market-oriented approach to farming. Pastures, heaths, fens, and marshes were drained and put to work, forests cut to create space for more fields.

Western peoples approached nature with less trepidation, more confidence. Scientists such as Galileo and Descartes reduced what had been a mysterious and daunting world to mathematics. The experimental method, not passive piety, made the world apprehensible. This optimism accelerated with the eighteenth-century Enlightenment, a movement, as its name implies, suffused with a spirit of confidence in the ability of human beings to fathom and manipulate their world. Progress in abstract and practical science validated this growing faith in human reason and intellect. Christians had previously understood dominion over the earth as an unmerited gift from God. Now that dominion, made much more complete, was their own hard-won achievement. God had become a remote entity that set the universe in motion and then stood aside as people seized their futures. Practical men of the eighteenth and early nineteenth centuries created machines for spinning and weaving cotton, harnessing steam, harvesting crops, and casting metals, all of which multiplied the rate at which food, minerals, and wood were extracted from the earth and bent to human will.

But growing numbers of Europeans realized that their new machines and techniques could endanger the very prosperity they had fostered. Agriculture had less to do with subsistence, with feeding local populations, more to do with generating money by producing crops for distant markets. But these shifts put more pressure on the land. Thoughtful farmers compensated by rotating crops more carefully, using legumes such as peas and clover to restore nitrogen to depleted soils, for example.

Others worried about the consequences of shrinking forests. Sixteenth-century landslides and floods provoked a ban on logging in parts of Florence. Germans began noticing wood shortages around 1600, and in the late eighteenth century they began regulating logging in an attempt to provide a reliable annual supply of firewood and building material. The first forestry school appeared in 1763 and was accompanied by many articles and books on the subject. 'From the State Forest not more and not less may be taken annually than is possible on the basis of good management by permanent sustained yield,' remarked a 1795 text.[2] The Danes created Forest Acts in 1763 and 1805, with the latter set of regulations requiring both preservation and replanting. Russia's reform-minded Peter the Great in the early eighteenth century touted forest preservation as a means to both slow erosion and ensure a reliable supply of oak trees for masts. The French expressed similar concerns as early as the

Peter the Great in the early eighteenth century touted forest preservation as a means to both slow erosion and ensure a reliable supply of oak trees for masts

twelfth century. Their Forest Ordinance of 1669, though routinely ignored, covered human activities from grazing and charcoal production to logging, even how many seed-bearing trees were to be left standing.

Forestry became not an exercise in cutting down trees as quickly as possible, but a process of establishing rational, even mathematical, equations to ensure that trees were utilized with maximum, long-term efficiency.

Forestry

The scientific and systematic management of forests emerged in Germany in the eighteenth century. The new field was primarily concerned with the rational use of timber. Wood constituted a precious military and economic resource, and foresters were charged with calculating rates of logging that would leave sufficient wood available for subsequent governments and generations.

In the nineteenth and early twentieth centuries foresters paid more attention to how forests prevented erosion and flooding and fostered healthy drinking water. They worked harder at preventing forest fires and replanting logged areas. Modern foresters often describe trees not just as crops to be cultivated and harvested, but as part of an ecosystem supporting a complex and interrelated set of organisms.

This emphasis on conservation, on using natural resources in a sustainable manner, flew in the face of western tradition and local demands, but it fitted well the requirements of the new science and the modern economy. Trees could best be understood as timber, as material to be converted into fuel, fences, houses, and railroad ties. Like the earth itself, they were expansive yet finite and ought therefore to be used judiciously. Empirical study and mathematical equations should determine the rate at which they should be cut and the uses to which they should be put. Forestry was a scientific study in which specially trained humans used reason to address concrete, practical problems.

Natural history in some ways resembled forestry. The rational exploitation of the earth's flora and fauna, after all, required an exhaustive cataloguing of those commodities. Botanists and other collectors commonly accompanied explorers such as Captain James Cook because the sponsors of such expeditions wanted to know the commercial and agricultural potential of distant lands that they hoped to colonize.

But by the eighteenth century a growing array of enthusiastic amateurs who gathered plants and insects in the fields and hills around their homes had joined the self-conscious professionals. These collectors eventually formed natural history societies, such as the British Association for the Advancement of Science. British publishers produced books on natural history that sold very, very well in the nineteenth century, and British newspapers included natural history sections. 'By the middle of the century, there was hardly a middle-class drawing-room in the country that did not contain an aquarium, a fern-case, a butterfly cabinet, a seaweed album, a shell collection, or some other evidence of a taste for natural history . . .'.[3] Natural history collecting and societies spread to Canada and other English colonies.

These collectors were fired by several impulses, not all of them instrumental. The amateurs, to be sure, believed that they were advancing scientific knowledge. They fitted their discoveries into an interminable Linnaean catalogue of nested classification in which plants, animals, and minerals were assigned places in an extensive but fixed hierarchy. Status accrued to those who assembled and organized the most specimens and facts. Unlike twentieth-century ecologists, they were not much interested in how their insects or plants fitted with the rest of the environment. This interest in the jots and tittles, the genus and species, of beetles and ferns embodied the Enlightenment confidence that nature could be, literally, pinned down, that it could be sorted and contained in a finite, if vast, system of kingdoms,

Discovering, describing, and cataloguing the world's flora and fauna represented Europeans' growing sense of mastery over the natural world

classes, and genera. Nature was a static collection of species and data that could and would be fully defined, not a dynamic set of interactions. Discovering, describing, and cataloguing the world's flora and fauna represented Europeans' growing sense of mastery over the natural world.

Yet amateur naturalists also looked backward, to a time when nature constituted not a scientific laboratory, but God's handiwork. They were apt to be pious Protestants, particularly Quakers, for whom plants, insects, and shells suggested the beautiful, intricate, and wondrous work of God's creation, 'through Nature up to Nature's God,' as British collectors liked to put it.[4]

European gardens illustrated the same ambivalence over man's growing power. By the time of the Reformation, in the 1520s, Italians had the most elaborate and celebrated. Fine gardens spread north, with economic growth. Holland's urban elite purchased country estates in the seventeenth century that they surrounded with elaborate arrangements of plants, especially foreign and flowering varieties. These gardens provided a foil to wild landscapes. They served not simply to please the eye, but to demonstrate how human artifice made nature orderly and pleasant.

Gardens also performed political functions. More than one historian has pointed out that the overwhelming Versailles gardens of Louis XIV, which consumed more water than the 600,000 denizens of Paris, were meant to suggest that a monarch who could so successfully control nature should also control his nation. The ability to make a thousand flowers bloom betokened a sort of supernatural command of the rest of creation. Likewise, the tree-lined avenues leading up to important people's homes connoted power as well as taste.

Yet the unprecedented wealth of the eighteenth century was accompanied by gardens that were not only larger, but less orderly. Geometric and rigid landscapes – patent in their human artifice – gave way to less linear arrangements of plants, hills, water, and temples. These gardens required a great deal of intervention, not only in planting and cultivating various types of vegetation, but also in fashioning the very features that lent the gardens such a 'natural' appearance. An English landscape garden created in 1764 included a forty-acre lake. Indeed, the fences that separated the gardens around British estates from the fields and woods (and cows) beyond them were sunken so as not to jar peoples' line of vision, to blur purposefully the division between two very different landscapes. From the windows of aristocratic homes, no discernible line separated the contrived and calculated nature of the garden from the relatively unkempt lands beyond them.

Eighteenth-century landscape gardens fed people's souls. The Duke of Buckingham wrote that 'the works of nature appear to me the better sort of sermons; and every flower contains in it the most edifying rhetorick, to fill us with the admiration of its omnipotent Creator.' A half century later, in 1755, writer Edward Young turned Milton on his head by asserting: 'A garden to the virtuous is a paradise still extant; a paradise unlost.'[5] As God became more remote, flowers and other domesticated plants became not simply tokens of the creator's blessings but

> *Growing numbers of well-to-do Britons alarmed religious authorities by choosing their gardens over their church yards as burial grounds*

emblems of perfection in and of themselves. Growing numbers of well-to-do Britons alarmed religious authorities by choosing their gardens over their church yards as burial grounds, as if to say that these places were their Eden, and their heaven, too.

Western Europe's leading artists and intellects embraced nature. Wordsworth, Keats, Shelley, Coleridge, Blake, Goethe, Balzac, Beethoven, Berlioz, Liszt, and Wagner turned to the non-human world for inspiration. Jean-Jacques Rousseau inaugurated the movement in the mid-eighteenth century when he turned the rational wing of the Enlightenment on its ear by celebrating 'primitive' people as authentic and independent precisely because they lived outside the artificiality and selfishness of civilized, urban life. 'I closed all my books,' explains one of his characters. 'There is one book open to all eyes, that of nature.'[6] Nature served to stimulate modern people's souls and imaginations, fostering a healthy, reflective individualism.

Indeed, individualism resided at the heart of this cult of nature loving. 'I rustle with the wind,' wrote German philosopher Johann Gottfried von Herder, 'and become alive – give life – inspire – I inhale fragrance, and exhale it with the flowers; I dissolve in water; I float in blue sky; *I* have all these feelings.'[7] The poet William Wordsworth believed that nature and human consciousness mirrored each other: '. . . what I saw/ Appeared like something in myself, a dream,/ A prospect in my

Jean-Jacques Rousseau, 1712–78

Born in Geneva, Switzerland to a family of modest means, Rousseau grew up in the care of an aunt and uncle before striking out on his own at the age of sixteen. He read widely and diligently and made his way to Paris in 1742, where Denis Diderot asked him to write some articles for his monumental *Encyclopédie*.

Rousseau produced a bevy of diverse and influential works: the *Discourse on the Origin and Foundation of Inequality Among Mankind*, *The New Heloise* (a novel), *Émile* (which presented his ideas on child rearing) and *Confessions*, his path-breaking autobiography.

Like other Enlightenment writers, Rousseau had an optimistic view of the human condition. He denied the religious and political orthodoxies of the day, that human beings were abject sinners incapable of thinking for or governing themselves.

But Rousseau broke from his intellectual peers in arguing that the blessings of civilization and progress were, at best, mixed. If humans were born free and perfect – or at least, perfectible – why were most civilized people so miserable? Rousseau reasoned that modern society had failed them on several scores, that it had become too contentious, unjust, and self-conscious, too stultifying and artificial. The antidote was to cultivate emotion and imagination, forces that lay beyond rationality.

Rousseau did not reject progress. Nature provided a counter-balance and corrective to civilization, not a negation of it. Remarks one of his characters of a beautiful garden: 'It is true that nature has created everything, but under my direction and there is nothing there which I have not ordered.'[8]

Persecuted for his writings and suspicious of his friends, Rousseau increasingly withdrew from conventional society and its concerns and embraced feeling and experience. He died on a summer morning, gazing out at a beautiful garden.

mind.'[9] Ludwig Van Beethoven, one of the era's consummate individualists, professed himself 'only happy in the midst of untouched nature.'[10] Romantics embraced the self and nature, the natural self.

William Wordsworth, 1770–1850

If Rousseau represented Romanticism's early shoots, Wordsworth constituted its florescence.

Born to a prosperous English family, Wordsworth exhibited a keen interest in the outdoors well before earning his college degree. Sponsored by a wealthy friend, he was soon able to devote himself to poetry and moved to the Lake District of England in 1799.

> *Wordsworth found in nature not a collection of substances to be studied and prodded and put to good use, but divinity itself*

Wordsworth found in nature not a collection of substances to be studied and prodded and put to good use, but divinity itself. *Tintern Abbey*, written and published in 1798, declared his allegiance. He was 'well pleased to recognize/ In nature and the language of the sense,/ The anchor of my purest thoughts, the nurse,/ The guide, the guardian of my heart, and soul/ Of all my moral being'.[11] Wordsworth's nature – and world – was not all sweetness and light. The French Revolution and much of the rest of the world had gone sour. The Enlightenment faith in human reason and rationality was perhaps misplaced. Perfect political institutions and understanding remained beyond humanity's grasp. Yet the contemplation of nature could and should be intensely and personally mystical and enlightening – a religious experience.

Wordsworth trod many thousands of miles in his beloved Lake District cultivating these sensibilities in himself and others. He died there a month after his last long walk.

Nature was not always agreeable. True, many aesthetes celebrated a pretty, picturesque, quaint nature. The movement peaked in the 1790s in England, where John Constable's paintings offered a harmonious palette of trees, fields, sky, and rural folk, a countryside shaped but hardly spoiled by humanity. But more and more artists turned from the picturesque to the sublime, from the pleasant to the forceful. Beethoven pioneered the use of dissonant, even sinister musical compositions, and his evocations of nature, as in his Sixth Symphony, featured a fearsome storm as well as pastoral themes. Wordsworth described solitary, dark pools surrounded by 'huge stones and masses of rock,' a vista that 'excites a sense of some repulsive power strongly put forth and thus deepens the melancholy natural to such scenes'.[12] Nature could be 'awful & immeasurable.' Likewise, the landscape painter J.M.W. Turner forsook pleasant British country scenes for indistinct, menacing representations. To capture the terror of a storm at sea he asked to be lashed to a ship's mast for several hours, an ordeal so awful that 'I did not expect to escape.'[13] The fear this experience induced is palpable in *The Slave Ship*, a painting in which indistinct sea monsters devour slaves that have been pitched from a vessel swallowed by malignant, squatting clouds.

Picturesque depictions of nature invited people to feel good about nature. The sublime, like other elements of the Romantic Movement, simply required them to feel – and strongly. In either event, nature provided a sanctuary that excised banal society so that the solitary, sensitive soul could connect with primal forces.

These ideas soon spread beyond artists and intellectuals. Intrigued by Rousseau's celebration of primitivism, Marie

Intrigued by Rousseau's celebration of primitivism, Marie Antoinette and her retinue played at being peasants in the gardens of Versailles

Antoinette and her retinue played at being peasants in the gardens of Versailles. The growing urban, middle class was particularly interested in celebrating nature. Mountains and seas had long been regarded as dreadful and threatening places unsusceptible to improvement. Now the burgeoning cities had become degraded and diseased, less populated places vivifying and restorative.

The search for pastoral peace created a rural tourist industry. By the 1780s guide books directed sensitive tourists to Rousseau's Hermitage, where he had written some of his most influential works. Germans flocked to the Rhineland for inspiration, a pilgrimage facilitated by steamship and then rail travel. 'Between Mainz and Cologne,' observed an engraver in 1840, 'hardly a house, hardly a tree can be found which has not set in motion a pen or a gouge.'[14] Wordsworth was hosting some 500 visitors annually to his home in the Lake District by the 1840s, where his poems instructed less articulate souls what to feel as they trekked across the landscape he had made famous.

Genteel tourists were soon worrying that their less-cultivated counterparts did not approach nature properly. Wordsworth wrote several editions of a guide book to his beloved Lake District between 1810 and 1842, which he hoped would be of use to 'the *Minds* of Persons of taste, and feeling for Landscape.'[15] But as growing numbers of travellers flocked northward, he fretted over 'cheap trains pouring out their hundreds at a time along the margin of Windermere,' that the countryside would soon be plagued by 'wrestling matches, horses and boat races without number.'[16]

The same thing was happening in North America. Niagara Falls, on the border of Canada and the US, moved from being 'the ultimate test of the "civilized" man or woman's ability to feel deeply . . . to hear Nature speak,' to a mere tourist destination. A writer in 1846 complained that the site was plagued with 'Chinese pagoda, menagerie, camera obscure, museum, watchtower, wooden monument, sea gardens, "curiosity shops".'[17]

European and especially English beaches were similarly transformed. The waters of mineral and hot springs had long been celebrated for their healing properties. By the early eighteenth century physicians were prescribing salt-water bathing. This recommendation, coupled with a growth in disposable incomes, brought a trickle and then a stream of vacationers to English resorts. The bathers were soon appreciating more than the ocean's water. Many, with ubiquitous guide books in hand, collected seashells or seaweed. Shells and pebbles could be arranged into intricate mementos of a stay at the beach. Other, more ambitious collectors, started (short-lived) aquariums.

The ocean itself drew many pilgrims. Its boundless expanses provided the anvil upon which artists and other aesthetes could forge their identities and refine their sensibilities. Fishing villages had turned their backs to the threatening sea, seeking refuge and vistas inland. But in the early nineteenth century resorts began staking out ground near the water's edge and installing large windows where visitors could absorb 'all the grandeur of the storm' while staying warm and dry.

As in Wordsworth's Lake District, more Spartan nature lovers lamented the commercialization of what they argued should be a more elemental experience. 'What are they doing here?' asked a man observing a group of stockbrokers at the seaside. 'If they had true relish of the ocean,' he wondered, 'why have they brought all this land luggage with them?.'[18]

But – then as now – nature loving and comfort in fact correlated more often than not. By the mid-nineteenth century, middle-class English families were going to the seaside for a month or more, soaking in the resplendent ocean even as they enjoyed most, if not all, of the amenities of home. By that date seaside resorts were also common in southern Europe and the eastern US. This would not be the first time that the people most insulated from nature's bite, people who had time and money on their hands, were the most apt to celebrate its beneficence and beauty.

Prosperity also reworked people's relationships with animals. Oxen, cattle, and other creatures had played a key role in the continent's economic transformation. By the fourteenth century the average European used much more animal power than his or her counterpart in China or Africa, let alone the Americas. But urbanization and economic growth removed a larger and larger proportion of people from direct contact with working animals. Pets stepped into the breach. Royal menageries expanded during the seventeenth century. Louis XIV kept ostriches, camels, elephants, crocodiles, and gazelles, animals from across the Mediterranean lands that he dominated. Like the elaborate gardens of

But urbanization and economic growth removed a larger and larger proportion of people from direct contact with working animals. Pets stepped into the breach

Versailles, such collections served political and imperial ends by suggesting the long reach of his power. Royals and aristocrats of the sixteenth and seventeenth centuries kept animals as pets, especially dogs, a practice that soon spread to the growing urban middle class. Dogs, cats, squirrels, monkeys, tortoises, otters, rabbits, mice, hedgehogs, toads, and a variety of birds made themselves at home among the bourgeois. Song birds were popular in London by the late seventeenth century.

Pets became quasi-family members. They typically lived indoors and might go to church. They seldom performed work and certainly were not to be eaten. Pets showed up in family portraits and graveyards, and not a few owners expected to meet their departed friends in heaven, since dogs had souls, too. Russian writers suggested that dogs committed suicide when their masters died.

The multiplication of pets engendered attempts at animal protection by the late eighteenth century in Great Britain. Some became so enamoured of birds that they abjured putting any type on their plates – and criticized their Italian and French counterparts for being so barbarous as to keep consuming them. The Society for the Prevention of Cruelty to Animals appeared in the 1820s in London and quickly gained influential members. Bullbaiting, the practice of setting dogs or other animals on bulls, was banned in 1835, cock-fighting in 1849. France's Society for Protection of Animals denounced bull-fighting and using dogs to pull carts.

The affinity of members of the middle class for animals, like their love of the outdoors, reflected their economic and social position. Lamenting animal cruelty served to criticize both the idle aristocracy for hunting and the struggling lower classes for

> ## Royal Society for the Prevention of Cruelty to Animals
>
> Founded in 1824 in London, this organization quickly gained the backing of influential people, and in 1840 Queen Victoria allowed the organization to include 'Royal' in its title. For several decades the society focused on encouraging the enforcement of legislation penalizing the abuse of animals, particularly farm and draft animals. The society successfully prosecuted 147 violators in its first year and by 1855 employed eight constables. It also lobbied law-makers and educated the public on animal welfare.
>
> During the second half of the nineteenth century, the RSPCA paid increased attention to pets, sporting (fighting) animals, and animal experimentation, though many of their members did not object to this last, scientific activity. The society spread to much of the British empire and plays an important role in animal rescue in many communities today.

abusing the animals on which their livelihoods depended. Popular forms of amusement like cock or dog fighting also offended the reformers. Blood sport was out of step with the emerging Victorian ethos of self-restraint and public order.

Prosperous animal lovers liked to point out that the lower classes should learn from, rather than exploit, animals, creatures that accepted their station in life and went about their work cheerfully, without complaint. Victorian animal lovers reserved their highest praise for creatures that exhibited the most subservience (dogs much more so than cats) or that performed the most beneficial work (horses). Elephants were one of the few wild animals to receive much respect, as they purportedly surrendered their freedom to work cheerfully for humans. If only servants could be so tractable.

Concern for animal welfare also constituted a platform from which the growing middle class could criticize the indolent rich. By the late eighteenth century country gentlemen were creating gargantuan

By the late eighteenth century country gentlemen were creating gargantuan cattle and oxen that could carry more and more meat

cattle and oxen that could carry more and more meat. The British were proud of consuming more flesh than their continental counterparts, particularly the French. Beef – on the plate or in the field – represented British superiority. But the fat-laden, monumental creatures that aristocrats produced stood for more narrow concerns: the wealth and magnificence of their owners. Indeed, less prosperous Britons found these creatures more grotesque than useful. They were incapable of sustained labour and produced gelatinous, unsavoury meat. These excrescences of aristocratic vanity were 'a collection of agricultural luxuries' fattened by 'Dukes and Earls' who 'can afford a fancy, whether it is the purchase of a Titian, or the production of a prize bullock.' A clergyman criticized the practice from even higher moral ground and wondered if the creation and showing of animals suffering from 'overwhelming and torturing obesity' did not constitute a 'cruel and unchristian exhibition'.[19]

The growing concern for animals was circumscribed and conditional. Sympathy for the well-being of congenial dogs and horses was accompanied in England by a ruthless slaughter of those deemed deleterious to human endeavours: rats and moles, of course, but also badgers, hedgehogs, and foxes. Animals, like people, were expected to be useful.

Nature remained utilitarian in the colonies and nations created by Europeans. Settlers in the Americas and the Pacific were too concerned with overcoming nature to give much thought to protecting or celebrating it.

But the young US constituted something of an exception, not so much because of its growing prosperity, rather because of its distinctive and potent strain of nationalism.

Here, as in so many other fields, Thomas Jefferson played a crucial role. The Virginia planter was among the nation's most enthusiastic and skilled naturalists, and he itched to put the lie to George Louis Leclerc de Buffon's theory of American degeneracy. Buffon, the most celebrated naturalist of the day, found ample natural grounds for American inferiority. The unimpressive size of North America's mammals and the purported lack of agricultural and technological accomplishments by its indigenous peoples indicated that the continent could produce only 'cold men and feeble animals.'[20] Jefferson's *Notes on Virginia*, written during the American Revolution, countered this theory. Did not American bears, for example, weigh twice as much as their European counterparts? Jefferson went so far as to send Buffon a large panther skin and later, while in Paris, the skeleton of an American moose. If bigger were better, the new nation had nothing to be ashamed of.

These sorts of sentiments multiplied after the US achieved its independence. Clearly the young nation could not compete with its European counterparts in the conventional measures of civilization: art and architecture. But America's weakness, its newness, could be made a virtue. 'What are the temples which Roman robbers have reared, – what are the towers in which feudal oppression has fortified itself, – what are the

blood-stained association of the one, or the despotic supersti-
tions of the other, to the deep forests which the eye of God has
alone pervaded, and where Nature, in her unviolated sanctuary,
has for ages laid her fruits and flowers on His altar!' enthused a
patriot in 1833.[21] 'Nature's nation's' want of cathedrals and
castles underscored its innocence and virtue, its democracy. Its
unsurpassed forests and mountains offered proof enough of God's
favour – and a fresh canvas on which God's chosen people would
create the mightiest and best nation of all, the New Jerusalem.

That God's chosen nation was ploughing up, cutting down,
and otherwise subduing the very wilderness that distinguished it
was an irony lost on the young country's patriots. In the century
following the American Revolution they quickly spread across
the continent, laying waste to forests, grasslands, predators,
and other animals with good cheer and industry. It would not be
the last time that nature's loudest partisans would be its most
ambitious destroyers.

Nature conservation was much more developed in western
Europe by the mid-nineteenth century. Germany and other
nations had by then realized that a reliable supply of timber
required active management by specialized scientists – foresters
– who would determine the time and place and rate of harvesting
and a substantial bureaucracy to enforce forestry laws.

But most expressions of concern over and affinity for nature
were less calculated and logical. Natural history societies
devoted to the collection and exhibition of nature's bounty
dotted western Europe and some of its colonies. Pets and
gardens were commonplace, especially in England, where people
inside and outside the Royal Society for the Prevention of
Cruelty to Animals were lamenting the suffering of some

Natural history societies devoted to the collection and exhibition of nature's bounty dotted western Europe and some of its colonies

animals. Educated Christians no longer feared the rugged mountains and seashores but sought from them, in paintings and on vacation, meaning and transcendence.

The sprawling landscape gardens of British and Welsh country estates perhaps best expressed the paradoxical relationship between conservation and efficiency on the one hand and nature appreciation on the other. The owners of such estates made their bread and butter – not to mention their ample fortunes – by enclosing what had once been marginal land used by villages. Sometimes they absorbed and destroyed even the villages themselves. The profit-minded capitalists cultivated these expanded fields more intensively and turned many forests into tree plantations of rapidly growing softwoods, such as larch and pine.

But the casual eye would not have detected these enterprises from the windows of the manor house. These domestic views were carefully constructed to include broad expanses of lawn, noble oaks, placid lakes, perhaps some faux ruins evoking ancient Rome. A few cattle grazed in the distance, near a church steeple or, better yet, the crumbling walls of an old castle.

Like the residents of expensive beach homes at the turn of the twenty-first century, the owners of these estates drew a thick line between the increasingly commercialized and rationalized nature that supported their prosperity and the nature of the drawing room, garden, library, concert hall, and vacation destination. Nature provided both wealth and a counterbalance to wealth.

That is why nature-loving advanced most quickly in England, the nation that had most fully subdued it, among people of ample education and leisure who were most insulated from its vagaries.

This ironic relationship between material progress and nature loving would become more widespread and intense in the century preceding World War II. Western people would have more reasons than before to conserve nature for purposes that were both rational and irrational, economic and spiritual.

Recommended reading

Surveys of ideas about nature include: Clarence J. Glacken, *Traces on the Rhodian Shore: Nature and Culture in Western Thought from Ancient Times to the End of the Eighteenth Century* (Berkeley, CA: University of California Press, 1967); Peter Coates, *Nature: Western Attitudes since Ancient Times* (Berkeley, CA: University of California Press, 1998); Ramachandra Guha, *Environmentalism: A Global History* (Oxford: Oxford University Press, 2000).

Keith Thomas's *Man and the Natural World: A History of the Modern Sensibility* (New York: Pantheon, 1983) is outstanding. More specialized but useful studies include: Lynn Barber, *The Heyday of Natural History, 1820–1870* (Garden City, NY: Doubleday, 1980); Louise E. Robbins, *Elephant Slaves and Pampered Parrots: Exotic Animals in Eighteenth-Century Paris* (Baltimore: The Johns Hopkins University Press, 2002); D.G. Charlton, *New Images of the Natural in France: A Study in European Cultural History, 1750–1800* (Cambridge: Cambridge University Press, 1984); Tamara L. Whited, *Forests and Peasant Politics in Modern France* (New Haven, CT: Yale University Press, 2000); Paula Findlen, *Possessing Nature: Museums, Collecting, and Scientific*

Culture in Early Modern Italy (Berkeley, CA: University of California Press, 1994); Sarah Howell, *The Seaside* (London: Studio Vista, 1974). Romantic artists' views of nature are addressed by: Newton P. Stallknecht, *Strange Seas of Thought: Studies in William Wordsworth's Philosophy of Man and Nature* (Bloomington, IN: Indiana University Press, 1958); A.S. Byatt, *Wordsworth and Coleridge in their Time* (London: Nelson, 1970); Matthew Brennan, *Wordsworth, Turner, and Romantic Landscapes: A Study of the Traditions of the Picturesque and the Sublime* (Columbia, SC: Camden House, 1987); Ann Bermingham, *Landscape and Ideology: The English Rustic Tradition, 1740–1860* (Berkeley, CA: University of California Press, 1986).

Notes

1　Glacken, C.J. (1967) *Traces on the Rhodian Shore: Nature and Culture in Western Thought from Ancient Times to the End of the Eighteenth Century.* Berkeley, CA: University of California Press, pp. 464–5.

2　Rubner, H. (1984) 'Sustained Yield Foresty in Europe and its Crisis During the Era of Nazi Dictatorship,' in H.K. Steen (ed.), *History of Sustained-Yield Forestry: A Symposium.* NP: Forest History Society, p. 171.

3　Barber, L. (1980) *The Heyday of Natural History, 1820–1870.* Garden City, NY: Doubleday, p. 13.

4　Lowe, P.D. (1983) 'Values and Institutions in the History of British Nature Conservation,' in A. Warren and F.B. Goldsmith (eds.), *Conservation in Perspective.* Chichester, John Wiley & Sons, p. 333.

5　Coffin, D.R. (1994) *The English Garden: Meditation and Memorial.* Princeton, NJ: Princeton University Press, pp. 67, 69.

6　Gay, P. (1977) *The Enlightenment: An Interpretation, The Science of Freedom.* New York, NY: W.W. Norton, p. 547.

7 Cartmill, M. (1993) *A View to Death in the Morning: Hunting and Nature through History*. Cambridge, MA: Harvard University Press, p. 116.

8 Charlton, D.G. (1984) *New Images of the Natural in France: A Study in European Cultural History, 1750–1800*. Cambridge: Cambridge University Press, p. 36.

9 Brennan, M. (1987) *Wordsworth, Turner, and Romantic Landscape: A Study of the Traditions of the Picturesque and the Sublime*. Columbia, SC: Camden House, p. 55.

10 Schauffler, R.H. (1933) *Beethoven: The Man Who Freed Music*. Garden City, NY: Doubleday, Doran, p. 261.

11 Gill, S. (ed.) (1984) *William Wordsworth*. Oxford: Oxford University Press, p. 134.

12 Byatt, A.S. (1970) *Wordsworth and Coleridge in their Time*. London: Nelson, pp. 273–4.

13 Brennan, M. (1987) *Wordsworth, Turner, and Romantic Landscape: A Study of the Traditions of the Picturesque and the Sublime*. Columbia, SC: Camden House, pp. 79, 90.

14 Lekan, T.M. (2004) *Imagining the Nation in Nature: Landscape Preservation and German Identity,1885–1945*. Cambridge, MA: Harvard University Press, p. 26.

15 Buzard, J. (1993) *The Beaten Track: European Tourism, Literature, and the Ways to Culture, 1800–1918*. Oxford: Clarendon, p. 30.

16 Ousby, I. (1990) *The Englishman's England: Taste, Travel, and the Rise of Tourism*. Cambridge: Cambridge University Press, p. 192.

17 Jasen, P. (1995) *Wild Things: Nature, Culture, and Tourism in Ontario, 1790–1914*. Toronto: University of Toronto Press, pp. 33, 43.

18 Howell, S. (1974) *The Seaside*. London: Studio Vista, p. 46.

19 Ritvo, H. (1987) *The Animal Estate: The English and Other Creatures in the Victorian Age*. Cambridge, MA: Harvard University Press, pp. 72, 75.

20 Semonin, P. (2000) *American Monster: How the Nation's First Prehistoric Creature Became a Symbol of National Identity.* New York, NY: New York University Press, p. 125.

21 Nash, R.F. (2001) *Wilderness and the American Mind*, 4th edn New Haven, CT: Yale University Press, p. 73.

CHAPTER 2

Industrial nature loving

ONE CAN READ A LOT of books extolling the virtues of western environmentalism without running across the name of Hermann Göring. Yet the notorious Nazi leader expressed a great deal of affinity and concern for nature. Like many of his colleagues, including Hitler, he believed that German identity and strength resided in its natural landscape and that the nation's well being depended on the preservation of those features. A vegetarian, he hoped to somehow resuscitate aurochs, long extinct animals, and populate the woods of Lithuania and Poland with them.

Yet Göring was all for progress. He headed up a four-year plan to prepare Germany for war that entailed reclaiming more than 2 million hectares of undeveloped land for agriculture and increasing the timber cut by 50 to 60 per cent. The nation required, he remarked, 'not a natural forest, but rather a natural economic forest'.[1] He also commanded the Luftwaffe, the German air force, a key component in the most efficient war-making machine the world had yet seen.

31

> *Göring and other Nazi leaders venerated both natural landscapes and industrial growth*

Göring and other Nazi leaders venerated both natural landscapes and industrial growth. So did many other westerners.

The western world changed dramatically and irrevocably between the mid-nineteenth and mid-twentieth centuries. Industrialization and urbanization brought larger concentrations of people and much prosperity. Big factories spewed out a panoply of goods that railroads and then automobiles distributed far and wide.

Yet western peoples' approach to the environment still followed the path laid out in the eighteenth century. True, arguments for conserving natural resources became more numerous and persistent as those resources shrank, just as those concerned with the filth of western cities insisted that something had to be done about smoke. But the rising chorus of voices advocating nature preservation were more often concerned with humans' spiritual than material welfare. Even as more and more people relied more heavily than ever before on minerals, plants, and animals, they described themselves as turning to nature not for food, shelter, and clothing, but for succour. Nature loving more commonly embodied than contradicted material progress.

Industrialization's maw consumed an unprecedented amount of natural resources, and governments scrambled to balance production for the present with conservation for the future. France, where enforcement of ambitious forest laws had lagged, began overseeing its wood supply more effectively in the 1840s. Norway set aside and nurtured small pieces of forests starting in the late 1860s. Germany, long the world's leader in forest conservation, had over 2,000 members in its foresters' association by 1900. Great Britain paid a price for its intense logging and by 1900 was importing about 90 per cent of its softwoods. It began reserving much larger tracts of land and planting them with uniform species in the late nineteenth century. The Spanish government tried to limit logging and require replanting after World War I, though with limited success.

Conservation took longer to catch on in the US than in western Europe. New England's George Perkins Marsh had warned back in the 1840s that unfettered logging caused erosion and other problems. Marsh, who was no democrat, blamed these difficulties on the untrammelled individualism of North America's pioneers. He argued that humans should be sensitive to what nature required, that there existed a natural and potentially stable equilibrium that people should discern and facilitate. Logging in the European style and setting aside some areas for wilderness would well serve both wildlife and people in search of wild nature, and it would ensure a steady supply of logs and clean drinking water. Few people paid much attention to him. The first edition of *Man and Nature*, published in 1864, sold only about 1,000 copies.

The tide turned in the 1890s. Gifford Pinchot, who had studied forestry in France and Germany, became the federal government's leading forester in 1898. Pinchot spread the gospel of scientific forest management, including sustainable yield, fuller utilization of forest products, fire prevention, and reforestation. He charged government foresters with implementing good forestry practices. Theodore Roosevelt, who became president in 1903, agreed. By 1906 over 150 million acres, nearly 20 per cent of the nation's standing timber, was under federal control – though millions of Americans resented the fact. Fire suppression became widespread by the 1920s, reforestation a decade later.

Forest conservation proceeded fitfully in Australia, New Zealand, and Canada, where thinly populated lands seemed all too robust. By the 1870s some Australians worried that logging practices both wasted wood and degraded soils and water. New Zealand passed a Forest Act in 1874 that required each province to set aside 3 per cent of its land for government timber. But the law was repealed just two years later, the victim of popular fear of government and desire for development. By 1880 some lumbermen and foresters in eastern Canada favoured closer regulation of logging, though they made little headway.

Conservationists pointed out how unregulated logging brought erosion, climate change, and poor water. But their message of wise, calculated use flew in the face of economic individualism and opportunity

Conservationists pointed out how unregulated logging brought erosion, climate change, and poor water. But their message of wise, calculated use flew in the face of economic individualism and opportunity, ideals that had flourished throughout the western world and remained particularly potent in recently colonized areas.

Those concerned with urban environmental problems encountered the same sort of difficulties. A sanitary movement to improve western Europe's drinking and sewage systems arose in the middle of the nineteenth century, and in the coming decades the growing urban, middle-class citizens of Prussia and

Germany were spearheading a movement demanding that government provide these amenities. By 1914, 94 per cent of Prussian and German towns and cities had a central water supply.

But industrial pollution grew. Manchester, brimming with factories and residences, was covered by black soot by the century's close. 'The very birds of the air are tarred,' remarked an observer. But industrialists and workers alike associated smoke with prosperity. Poor people were reluctant to stop burning coal, which connoted comfort, and expressed suspicion over anti-pollution measures that might jeopardize their jobs. 'Wheer there's smook there's brass,' (money), they explained.[2] Conservation fared poorly when it appeared to threaten peoples' livelihoods, and effective pollution control would not appear until after World War II.

Urban parks did not much threaten the industrial status quo and were therefore established more easily. England began creating large numbers of them in the 1840s, and other western nations eventually followed suit. 'Let our children develop in sunshine and flowers,' proclaimed an Australian city planner.[3] British factory owners encouraged their employees to grow vegetables and flowers, and the gardens of the well-to-do continued to increase in number and size. 'The enjoyment to be derived from a suburban residence depends principally,' wrote the British author of *The Suburban Gardener*, 'on a knowledge of the resources which a garden, however small, is capable of affording.'[4] Later in the century advocates of garden cities called for widely spaced suburban homes separated by ample woods, an arrangement that only the very prosperous could achieve.

Many wanted to make a garden out of entire swaths of the British countryside. In 1850 half of England was urban. In 1921 the proportion had soared to 80 per cent. Anti-industrialists such as John Ruskin, John Morris, and Edward Carpenter advocated a literal return to the rural past, for agricultural communes and manual labour. This pre-industrial economy would recreate a pre-modern and virtuous economy. Hence Morris celebrated medieval architecture as 'the outcome of corporate and social feeling, the work not of individual but collective genius; the expression of a great body of men conscious of their union.'[5] Less ideological Britons also embraced the countryside. Industrialization, the broad set of processes that had drawn so many to cities, both provided the means to travel from the city to the countryside (railroads and then automobiles) and the motive (a desire to escape a society that was becoming more comfortable and mechanized). Rural England's fields, forests, and old buildings became 'a special source of value: an organic place, one of continuity and organic accumulation and of enduring values' that counterbalanced the 'disorder and false values' of the city.[6] 'There is sublimity in every hedgerow,' asserted one early devotee.[7] England's economic power resided in its manufacturing centres, its military power in its navy. But its soul was to be found in rural lanes.

Rural England's fields, forests, and old buildings became 'a special source of value: an organic place, one of continuity and organic accumulation and of enduring values'

Wild places represented nationalism in former colonies. The US had identified itself as nature's nation soon after gaining its independence. Urban, middle-class Canadians were taking to the woods in large numbers by the twentieth century's turn, at a cabin by a lake or, as a writer in *Man-to-Man Magazine* hoped, tracking bears or mountain goats with 'a real gun . . . strapped over your shoulder . . . making your way through a God-made wilderness.'[8] Canada's geography, particularly its boundless north, bequeathed to it a distinct, masculine identity which set it apart from the mother country. 'As long as the north wind blows, and the snow and sleet drive over the forests and fields,' remarked a patriot, 'we must be a hardy, a virtuous, a daring, and if we are worthy of our [purportedly Nordic] ancestors, a dominant race.'[9] By the late nineteenth century many well-to-do urban Australians were self-consciously styling themselves as 'bushwalkers' who sought 'the canyons, ranges, and wildest parts of this country.'[10] Regeneration came not from English culture or manufactures but in the Australian bush. 'The New Zealand forest looks best when no foreign element intrudes,' a politician explained in 1903, adding 'European and American trees that are very beautiful in themselves do not always look well among those of New Zealand.'[11]

Germans had long forged nationalism in the bowels of nature. 'The German people need the wood as man needs the wine,' asserted Wilhelm Heinrich Riehl in the mid-nineteenth century. The Rhine River was particularly beloved, and Germans were willing to spill blood to control its banks. Soldiers marched to battle in the Franco-Prussian War in 1870 singing *The Watch on the Rhine*. Early twentieth-century intellectuals such as Thomas Mann and Hermann Hesse described the creation of nature parks as 'a truly patriotic deed!' The Friends of Nature, 30,000 strong by 1914, argued that nature offered a model of freedom for the working class – their slogan: 'Free Mountains, Free World, Free People.' This association of nature with

Germany's essence opened the door for chauvinism or worse. German imperialists justified their domination of colonial peoples and places by arguing that their rule ensured more productive and sustainable practices. By the same token, the emigration of purportedly inferior peoples to Germany threatened both the nation's identity and its environment. An essay for the Nature Park Society blamed pollution on an 'unwashed brood of Croats and Pollacks' said to be shouldering aside Germany's 'flaxen-haired and blue-eyed boys and girls.'[12]

The Nazis paired nature loving with racism more consistently and patently. They believed that Germany's spirit sprang from its soil and woods and that their programme of racial superiority and purification was a natural process, not a cultural invention. Germany could flourish only if it preserved and created the environment in which its essence, its strength, resided. Blood and soil were one. Hence the purportedly inferior, Slavic lands to the east would be transformed into forested, German-like landscapes as German colonizers pushed aside purportedly inferior Slavic peoples.

With the exception of dogs, deemed loyal and fierce, the Nazis criticized pets, which they associated with soft sentimentality, the very sort of trait they hoped to purge from the Aryan race. They praised wild animals, particularly the wolf, thought to be without peer in fierceness and courage. Hitler commonly referred to himself as a wolf.

The Nazis did not just talk about nature. Under their rule Germany became the first modern nation to safeguard wolves, and they created the strongest animal-protection law in the world. (They associated animal cruelty with Judaism, claiming that kosher butchering prolonged the suffering of dying animals.) The Nazis created hundreds of nature preserves and thousands of natural monuments.

None of this much interfered with the Nazis' relentless industrial and technological development. A forest overseer who objected to soldiers drilling in a protected area was branded a 'communist.' The autobahn completed in 1939 provided views of mountains, lakes, and ruins, and its curvilinear features suggested harmony with the rest of the landscape. 'The straight line does not stem from nature,' explained a designer.[13] But it was no less an engine of economic and military development for that.

The Nazis' opposite number, Soviet communists, evinced a much less romantic view of the landscape. Russia's conservationists were soon on the defensive after the Bolsheviks came to power. Lenin had long enjoyed the outdoors. But he and other leaders were obsessed with efficiency and production. The Soviet Union established the nation's first park, or *zapovedniki*, in 1920,

> *Lenin had long enjoyed the outdoors. But he and other leaders were obsessed with efficiency and production*

and it soon added more. But these parks served narrow, utilitarian ends. Here, it was hoped, scientists could discern both the 'carrying capacities of nature' and provide space for commercially valuable species to recover. Conservationists who pronounced these goals too narrow invited censure. Stalin was even more preoccupied with immediate productivity than Lenin had been, and his first five-year plan called for 'the great transformation of nature.' A writer depicted the great leader considering a map of the Karelia Republic: 'Primeval forests. Too much forest as a matter of fact; it covers the best soil. And swamps. The swamps are always crawling about, making life dull and slovenly. Tillage must be increased. The swamps must be drained.' Intellectuals concerned with how this affected the environment could find themselves condemned for indulging in 'apoliticism,' with living in a sort of 'zapovedniv for the Endangered Species of Bourgeois Scientists.' The editors of the field's leading journal prudently changed its name from *Conservation* to *Nature and the Socialist Economy*, and the All-Russian Society for Conservation became Promotion of the Growth of Natural Resources. An editorial forsook 'the old tendencies of "conservation of nature" for the sake of nature itself.'[14] The *zapovedniki* survived until the 1950s, but were used for grazing, mining, logging, and to host exotic animals that might prove useful.

The Soviets' association of nature preservation with the bourgeois was nearly as accurate as it was self-serving. Australia's early bushwhacker clubs were patently elitist. The Mountain Trails Club, formed in 1914, admitted just fifty-five members in its first fifty-six years – all of them men. Educated men across the western world asserted a special claim to camping and other outdoor activities. Prosperous males, it seemed, had been enervated by progress. 'No nation facing the unhealthy softening and relaxation of fibre that tends to accompany civilization can afford to neglect anything that will develop hardihood, resolution, and the scorn of discomfort and danger,' asserted Theodore Roosevelt.[15] Military service and rugged sports – rugby and cricket in the British Commonwealth, boxing and American football in the US – could provide the danger and violence that everyday life had once offered. So could the outdoors. The Boy Scouts began in England in 1907 and quickly spread to Australia and the US, where it was soon the nation's largest youth organization. The associated woodcraft movement, defined by one proponent as 'the art of getting along well in the wilderness by utilizing nature's storehouse,' was very popular from the 1890s to the 1930s.[16]

But white people made it clear that the wilderness would not interfere with civilization. Armchair adventurers regaled themselves with male adventure novels, including the exploits of Tarzan, a white Englishman raised by apes who somehow incorporated nature's virility without losing his civilized essence – or his superiority to Africans. In the 1920s many Caucasians overcame their fear of dark skin sufficiently to sunbathe for the first time. Yet they continued to insist that dark-skinned peoples possessed an insufficient understanding of nature, that they both failed to develop their natural resources and to protect the big-game animals that Europeans liked to hunt.

Working people commonly opposed conservation and pre-servation. More than one in five residents of the Palatinate were arrested annually from 1830 to 1845 for stealing wood or otherwise violating its forest laws, regulations that bore heavily on poor residents who used the woods for fuel, food, and forage. Plans to transform the pastures of Auzat, France into forests prompted its residents to lament the prospect of 'no flocks, no fertilizer, no harvests, nothing at all in fact, if not flight or death.'[17] In the US, too, prosperous and marginal people sparred over environmental protection. The campaign to end the feather trade, the shooting of beautiful birds whose bodies adorned women's hats around the twentieth cen-tury's turn, associated this fashion choice with the 'real loidy who . . . with hat cocked over one eye, pink tie, scarlet waist . . .

> *The growing number of recreational hunters who shot wildlife denigrated those who killed such animals to feed their families as 'pot hunters,' vulgar men who did not give their prey a sporting chance*

haunts the cheaper shops . . . chews gum, and expectorates with seeming relish.'[18] The growing number of recreational hunters who shot wildlife denigrated those who killed such animals to feed their families as 'pot hunters,' vulgar men who did not give their prey a sporting chance. A burgeoning political force, the sport hunters lobbied to create and enforce laws that regulated and licensed hunters and set aside protected areas for game. Poorer, rural residents who used these same animals to put food on their tables and much-needed coin in their pockets resisted such efforts. Taking wild meat, an Alberta farmer explained, was 'the custom of every free-born son of the soil.'[19] 'Wild game, wild fish and wild birds belong to the people,' asserted a resident of the Adirondack Mountains of New York.[20] Wealthy outsiders such as William Rockefeller, J.P. Morgan, and Alfred Vanderbilt rubbed salt into the wounds of locals by establishing private parks where only they and their guests could hunt. Residents retaliated by tearing down 'no trespassing signs,' destroying fences, and shooting at game wardens or guards. They killed the owner of a private park.

The number and extent of public nature reserves and parks expanded dramatically in the century leading up to World War II. Several British groups formed to protect the countryside: the Federation of Rambling Clubs in 1905, the Councils for the Protection of Rural England and Rural Wales in 1926 and 1928,

National Trust

Founded in 1895 by prominent philanthropists, the National Trust soon became the leading organization devoted to preserving natural and historical landscapes in Great Britain. Unlike preservationists in North America and Australia, the Trust focused on places that had been heavily shaped by human – though usually pre-industrial – hands.

By 1938 it protected about 45,000 acres. Two decades later it owned more than 130 historic buildings and had 65,000 members. Its acreage and membership soared again from the 1960s. In 2004 the National Trust controlled 612,000 acres. Though often overshadowed in public debates by more radical groups, its membership of over 3 million indicates its abiding influence.

respectively, and a Youth Hostels Association (for rural lodging) in 1930. The National Trust for England and Wales began conserving rural landscapes in the 1890s, and England established a National Parks Commission soon after World War II. These organizations succeeded in preserving both selected bits of countryside and walkers' access to rural places.

Denmark also removed land from agricultural or industrial production. Lightly populated West Jutland had been the target of ambitious development programmes for much of the nineteenth century, but by the century's turn these endeavours were criticized for moving 'like an iron roller over this beautiful and unique landscape,' for fostering 'the crassest materialism.' The Danes shifted from trying to integrate the marshy heaths into the national economy to treating them as 'a fairy tale land' set aside for nostalgia and other forms of recreation.[21]

Other European nations followed suit. France established its first national park in 1914, high in the mountains near Grenoble. Its stated purpose was to 'conserve and protect against all destruction, deterioration or disfiguration by man, the natural elements, fauna, flora, picturesque sites and distinctive geological and hydrological formations.'[22] Spain created its first national park in 1917 and established a list of protected Natural Areas of National Interest and Catalogue of Notable Trees.

Nature lovers in younger nations focused their attentions on wilderness preservation. 'Heaven grant that we may be able to retain many solitary places in this beautiful island of ours where nature in all her grandeur will reign supreme,' wrote a devotee of the Tasmanian backcountry, who hoped to keep such sacred places forever free from 'sulphur fumes, and axes and jam tins.'[23] The Royal National Park was established in 1879, near Sydney, Australia. Canada established parks in its breathtaking Rocky Mountains in the 1880s.

The US led the world in creating national parks. In 1864 the federal government granted the Yosemite Valley to California as a park. Eight years later it created Yellowstone National Park, which began as a collection of natural curiosities, a tourist attraction touted by the Northern Pacific Railroad. But in the 1880s Congress astonished many observers by refusing to let mining interests develop it. New Jersey's William McAdoo explained: 'Civilization is so

The US led the world in creating national parks. In 1864 the federal government granted the Yosemite Valley to California as a park. Eight years later it created Yellowstone National Park

universal that man can only see nature in her majesty and primal glory, as it were, in these as yet virgin regions.'[24] Many other expansive national parks would follow. The number of visitors to US national parks increased from less than 70,000 in 1908 to 335,000 in 1915. Nature's nation had become determined to preserve and enjoy parts of its wild scenery.

The young US produced passionate advocates for wilderness. Not many paid New England's Henry David Thoreau much heed when he proclaimed that 'in Wildness is the preservation of the World' in 1851, and not many read *Walden*, his most sustained account of nature, when it appeared three years later.[25] Thoreau's mentor, Ralph Waldo Emerson, enjoyed a wider audience. Emerson was a leading transcendentalist who believed, like Wordsworth, that God was immanent in nature, that humans could intuit God and truth through the contemplation of nature. Like most of his peers, he found walks through the countryside outside Boston sufficient to satisfy this urge. Thoreau, though put off by exposure to wild, uninhabited landscapes, desired a more intense interaction. He spent over two years at Walden Pond, where he observed the world around him, tended his beans, wrote in his journal, and pondered the relationships between humans and the rest of the world. Thoreau distrusted the American mania for speed and growth and busyness and found at Walden an antidote. 'Let us spend one day as deliberately as Nature,' he counselled, 'and not be thrown off the track by every nutshell and mosquito's wing on the rails.' Nature offered not simply a respite from frantic commerce and progress, but intimations of a different and compelling way of living. 'Shall I not have intelligence with the earth? Am I not partly leaves and vegetable mould myself?.'[26]

Like Rousseau before him, Thoreau did not reject the core values of western civilization, did not literally counsel a return to the woods. Rather, he wished those ideals to be buffered, to be chastened, by the other, less rational and more primitive, components of human nature.

The ideas explored by Thoreau gained traction late in the century. Indeed, John Muir found Thoreau's nature too tame and sought out wilderness, places seemingly untouched my human hands. Like Thoreau, he believed that 'civilized man chokes his soul.' Forests and mountains offered a balm. 'Nature's peace will flow into you as the sunshine into the trees. The winds will blow their freshness into you, and the storms their energy, while cares will drop off like autumn leaves.' Wilderness embodied God. Of the Sierra Mountains he remarked: 'everything in it seems equally divine – one smooth, pure, wild glow of Heaven's love.'[27]

Many followed him – by seeking out remote mountains or, more commonly, by reading his many articles in popular magazines. 'Thousands of tired, nerve-shaken, over-civilized people are beginning to find out that going to the mountains is going home,' enthused Muir.[28]

Yet western peoples brought to their parks and other protected areas the urban culture they were purportedly seeking to escape. Automobiles and buses eased access to the British countryside, even as they compromised the very tranquillity that their occupants sought. Ugly billboards, petrol stations and telephone boxes dotted the roadside, though Boy Scout troops made the latter less offensive by planting small gardens around them. Others found even the visitors' persons unsightly: 'sweating girls in shorts that enlarge without enhancing their charms.'[29]

John Muir, 1838–1914

Often paired with Thoreau and Leopold in the trinity of US environmentalism, Muir moved with his family from Scotland to the Wisconsin frontier in 1849. In college he traded in his Calvinism for transcendentalism. In 1867, after losing an eye while working in a carriage factory, he resolved to seek wilderness while he could still see it. He hiked from Indiana to the Gulf of Mexico before settling in California, where he became entranced by the Sierra Mountains. In the 1870s he began writing scores of articles for popular magazines and emerged as the world's leading prophet of wilderness.

Muir did not like to dwell on the bloodier aspects of nature, on death, competition, and destruction. But, unlike Thoreau, he coveted uncouth wilderness, and, unlike most nature lovers, he also asserted the intrinsic importance of all creatures, including rattlesnakes and coyotes, regardless of whether people found them useful or appealing.

Muir, who liked to preach 'these mountains like an apostle,' became very active in politics and was instrumental in making his beloved Yosemite a National Park in 1890.[30] He was the president of the Sierra Club for its first twenty-two years and led scores of people into the California backcountry. He tried, with little success, to convince Pinchot and Roosevelt to preserve for posterity rather than simply conserve for wise use more federal land. But Muir's unstinting literary and political efforts multiplied the number of people concerned about wilderness.

Tourism shaped the nature of even remote parks, as planners decided which landscape elements to accent or disguise, create or destroy. North American managers introduced exotic species and routinely poisoned and shot wolves, coyotes, mountain lions, hawks, and other predators well into the twentieth

Tourism shaped the nature of even remote parks, as planners decided which landscape elements to accent or disguise, create or destroy

century. They also tried to excise indigenous peoples, whose long-standing presence in places such as Yellowstone violated Caucasian expectations of wilderness.

Park managers hesitated to stand in the way of economic progress. Canada's tolerated logging and mining. Australia's Royal National Park was intended as much for recreation as preservation and included a zoo. New Zealand bureaucrats assured citizens that they did not 'with hold from settlement areas of rich soil . . . well adapted to pastoral or agricultural pursuits merely because they are also suited for scenery preservation.'[31] Scenery preservation, moreover, was no end in itself. The Superintendent of the Department of Tourist and Health Resorts defended leaving uncut the forest along the rail line stretching from Wellington to Auckland because it would 'afford a great attraction to travellers . . . whereas miles of burnt and blackened logs would prove a weariness to the spirit.'[32]

Wilderness preservation and nature for its own sake, though eloquently advanced by Muir, would not make much headway until well after World War II. Western people domesticated the very landscapes whose primitiveness they celebrated.

Domestication of animals also proceeded rapidly. Pet ownership continued to grow in the late nineteenth and early twentieth centuries, as more and more people associated animals with leisure rather than work or food. Dog shows became widespread in England after 1865 and helped fuel the creation of dozens of new breeds. Human intervention in genetics, from wheat to plough horses, was of course nothing new. But the creators of new varieties of dogs made no pretence of serving any practical purpose.

Undomesticated animals increasingly served intangible ends, too. Britons began tending to wild birds late in the nineteenth century, first leaving out crumbs during cold spells then building feeders, baths, and houses for their little friends. Beatrix Potter's drawings faithfully rendered rabbits, squirrels, and other creatures even as her prose described them acting very much like humans. Her children's books blended 'scientific knowledge and fablelike stories;' her characters 'live in a never-never land somewhere between people and real-life animals.'[33] Ethel Pedley dedicated *Dot and the Kangaroo* in 1899 to Australia's children 'in the hope of enlisting their sympathies for the many beautiful, amiable, and frolicsome creatures of their fair land.'[34] Pedley's creatures earned such sympathy. One, a mother kangaroo, rescued a little girl who had become lost in the bush. Anna Sewell's *Black Beauty*, a best-selling English novel termed 'the Uncle Tom's Cabin of the Horse,' had in 1877 jump-started a genre populated by noble animal protagonists.[35] Canada's Ernest Thompson Seton's *Wild Animals I Have Known* appeared in 1898 and also attracted a wide readership. Seton and other writers, such as William J. Long and Sir Charles G.D. Roberts, depicted wild animals as being very much like humans. Birds made casts to heal broken bones. In Seton's words, animals possessed 'the virtues most admired in Man,' including dignity, sagacity, obedience, and fidelity. Long transported readers to the 'School of the Woods' which offered 'a wholesome, cheerful life to make one glad and send him back to his own school with deeper wisdom

Beatrix Potter, 1866–1943

This Englishwoman has long been known for her whimsical children's stories featuring mischievous rabbits, squirrels, and hedgehogs. But her interest in nature ran much deeper than that.

Born to a prosperous family, Potter was privately educated and soon devoted to drawing, reading, and pets (including some bats) at a young age. She became a specialist in studying, cultivating, and painting mushrooms and fungi and hoped for recognition from England's scientific community. She prepared a paper to the Linnean Society in 1897, though, as a woman, she was not allowed to read it before that body.

> *Potter tired of trying to win acceptance in such a male-dominated field and turned to children's literature, where women were far more accepted*

Potter tired of trying to win acceptance in such a male-dominated field and turned to children's literature, where women were far more accepted. *The Tale of Peter Rabbit*, which she had written for an invalid child, was published in 1900, and others soon followed.

The charm of these stories resides in their capacity to both reaffirm and undermine conventional verities. Peter Rabbit spurns his mother's warnings and is nearly killed for it. But he survives to be comforted. Squirrel Nutkin's impertinence before Old Brown, the domineering owl, costs him only his tail, not his life. Potter of course illustrated her own books, and she based her highly realistic paintings and drawings on close observation of the animals around her – though this realism was sometimes compromised by human clothing or utensils.

A devotee of the English countryside, Potter left her property to the National Trust. Her books continue to persuade children and adults alike that animals are essentially human.

and renewed courage.'[36] Detractors scoffed at the 'nature fakers' outlandish stories. But the assertion that 'we and the beasts are kin' claimed millions of readers.[37]

Zoos were by this time making flesh-and-blood, exotic animals accessible to millions of urban residents across the western world. Jumbo the elephant was one of many celebrities of London's Regent's Park, and his sale to P.T. Barnum, the US showman, prompted a national outpouring of patriotic indignation.

Close familiarity with captured creatures bred, if not contempt, considerable condescension. The bear pit, in which the imposing mammals were made to beg for food, was a key component of late-nineteenth-century zoos: 'the animal that had long been associated with fear, the woods, and aristocratic hunting privileges was reduced in a controlled, urban, and bourgeois environment to a comic figure asked to perform for ladies, gentlemen, and perhaps most important, children.'[38]

This denatured and contrived relationship with animals – as pets, fictional protagonists, and zoo residents – was accompanied by a continued concern over how people treated certain animals. England's anti-cruelty movement had begun early in the nineteenth century, when it had focused on the abuse of domesticated and especially working animals. In the late nineteenth and early twentieth centuries reformers increasingly tried to protect wild animals. Birds received a great deal of attention. The Sea Birds Preservation Act of 1869 was the first piece of national legislation devoted to a particular species, and reformers across the western world soon criticized women for wearing hats featuring the feathers and carcasses of birds. Australians began passing laws protecting birds in 1901, though they were seldom enforced. England approved legislation safeguarding grey

Anthropomorphism

Anthropomorphism is the practice of imputing human characteristics and motives to non-humans. Christian Europe traditionally drew a thick line between man and animal, but that line began to blur with the spread of pets in the eighteenth century. Anthropomorphism surged with pet ownership, and by the turn of the twentieth century wild animals who spoke, wore clothes, and formed human-like families were common in children's and adult literature alike. These depictions prompted westerners to view animals in a much more positive light than before, though that affection rested on the mistaken assumption that these creatures thought and acted like people.

Ecologists and many environmentalists have attacked anthropomorphism in recent years as a token of humanity's inability to understand and respect other creatures on their own terms

Ecologists and many environmentalists have attacked anthropomorphism in recent years as a token of humanity's inability to understand and respect other creatures on their own terms. But the belief that animals are essentially people continues to shape western culture and environmental movements.

seals and badgers early in the twentieth century, and a 1921 act stopped the plumage trade.

Anthropomorphism continued to characterize western animal lovers. Bird devotees still referred to predators as 'cannibals.'[39] Early twentieth-century Australians centred concerns for wild animals on the koala, a cute, meek-appearing animal. 'It was humane sentiment and sentimentality that mobilized the Australian public, not the animal's place in Australian nature'.[40]

Nothing trumped motherhood for generating sentimentality, and the realization that many birds were mothers fired the campaign to end the feather trade. Traditionalists – and the milliners who created hats – could and did argue that nature was a source of beauty and that for lovely women to adorn themselves with nature's gifts was to pay nature a compliment. 'The earth and the sea give up their gems for her,' explained one man. 'Let the air do the same.' Practical-minded conservationists countered that birds ought to be left alive because they served humans by consuming insects. But saving birds so that they could kill bugs did not rally many to the cause. So Audubon Society members described how Florida hunters attacked snowy egret nests soon after their young had hatched, when mothers (devoted fathers generated little ink) were most reluctant to flee. 'When the killing is finished,' a writer explained, 'the slaughtered birds are left in a white heap to fester in the sun and wind in sight of their orphaned young that cry for food and are not fed.'[41] Women who wore white egret feathers were stained by the innocent blood of women and children.

But what was really being defended here, birds or motherhood, and did the preservation of either or both counter in the least humanity's growing subjection of the non-human world?

Nature loving had made considerable progress throughout the western world by the eve of World War II. Growing numbers of people – and not just intellectuals – spoke fondly of the untamed outdoors and sought respite and refreshment there. Nations created parks where their citizens could enjoy nature and, in some instances, restricted economic development that might compromise a landscape's primitive character. The gap between wild animals and humans narrowed as children and adults alike read stories depicting these creatures in a very favourable light. Audubon societies and other organizations formed to protect birds and other animals.

In the former colonies, especially, even the notion that natural resources should be consumed efficiently raised a firestorm of criticism

But nature loving hardly slowed the relentless course of western industrialization and progress. In the former colonies, especially, even the notion that natural resources should be consumed efficiently raised a firestorm of criticism. Preservationists, for their part, criticized conservationists such as Pinchot for allowing sheep to graze on federal land and countenancing a reservoir in the beautiful Hetch Hetchy Valley. But Muir's wide readership seldom translated into policies. Most preservationists and other nature enthusiasts, furthermore, pursued programmes that dovetailed rather than contradicted their economic interests. They were highly selective and favoured the protection of pieces of scenery deemed especially beautiful or picturesque, animal species defined as most akin to us. The growing cult of nature appreciation co-existed side by side with the industrial era's growing prosperity. Hence the narrator in a 1916 novel finds in a forest both a beauty reflecting God's glory and 'acres of the finest milling timber in New Zealand.'[42] Automobiles brought city dwellers to the suburbs, the countryside, and to parks. Hunting for sport rather than necessity, keeping animals as pets instead of food, even abjuring from wearing feathered hats served to demonstrate wealth and good taste.

The development of a substantial environmentalist movement that questioned rather than complemented the western programme of increased prosperity still lay well ahead by the eve of World War II.

Recommended reading

I.G. Simmons, *The Environmental History of Great Britain: From 10,000 Years Ago to the Present* (Edinburgh: Edinburgh University Press, 2001) contains some strong material on ideas. Kenneth Olwig's *Nature's Ideological Landscape: A Literary and Geographic Perspective on its Development and Preservation on Denmark's Jutland Heath* (London: George Allen & Unwin, 1984) is far-ranging and provocative. Other excellent specialized studies include: Harriet Ritvo's incisive *The Animal Estate: The English and Other Creatures in the Victorian Age* (Cambridge, MA: Harvard University Press, 1987); Nigel Rothfels, *Savages and Beasts: The Birth of the Modern Zoo* (Baltimore: The Johns Hopkins University Press, 2002); David Evans, *A History of Nature Conservation in Britain,* 2nd edn (London: Routledge, 1997); Stephen Mosley, *The Chimney of the World: A History of Smoke Pollution in Victorian and Edwardian Manchester* (Cambridge: White Horse Press, 2001); Barbara T. Gates, *Kindred Nature: Victorian and Edwardian Women Embrace the Living World* (Chicago: University of Chicago Press, 1998); Thomas M. Lekan, *Imagining the Nation in Nature: Landscape Preservation and German Identity, 1885–1945* (Cambridge, MA: Harvard University Press, 2004); Boria Sax, *Animals in the Third Reich: Pets, Scapegoats, and the Holocaust* (New York: Continuum,

2000). Raymond H. Dominick, III, *The Environmental Movement in Germany: Prophets and Pioneers, 1871–1971* (Bloomington, IN: Indiana University Press, 1992); Douglas R. Weiner, *Models of Nature: Ecology, Conservation and Cultural Revolution in Soviet Russia* (Indiana University Press, 1988) are detailed national studies.

The former colonies are surveyed in Thomas R. Dunlap, *Nature and the English Diaspora: Environment and History in the US, Canada, Australia, and New Zealand* (Cambridge: Cambridge University Press, 1999). Roderick Frazier Nash's magisterial *Wilderness and the American Mind*, 4th edn (New Haven, CT: Yale University Press, 2001) is indispensable. Other strong treatments of the US include: Samuel P. Hays, *Conservation and the Gospel of Efficiency: The Progressive Conservation Movement, 1890–1920* (Cambridge, MA: Harvard University Press, 1959); Ralph H. Lutts, *The Nature Fakers: Wildlife, Science & Sentiment* (Golden, CO: Fulcrum, 1990). Thoreau is treated in James McIntosh, *Thoreau as Romantic Naturalist: His Shifting Stance toward Nature* (Ithaca, NY: Cornell University Press, 1974), Thoreau and Marsh in Robert L. Dorman, *A Word for Nature: Four Pioneering Environmental Advocates, 1845–1913* (Chapel Hill, NC: University of North Carolina Press, 1998). Strong studies of Canada include: Carl Berger, *Science, God, and Nature in Victorian Canada* (Toronto: University of Toronto Press, 1983); Patricia Jasen, *Wild Things: Nature, Culture and Tourism in Ontario, 1790–1914* (Toronto: University of Toronto Press, 1995). Australia and New Zealand, respectively, are treated by: Drew Hutton and Libby Connors, *A History of the Australian Environment Movement* (Cambridge: Cambridge University Press, 1999); Eric Pawson and Tom Brooking, eds, *Environmental Histories of New Zealand* (Victoria, Australia: Oxford University Press, 2002).

Notes

1 Lekan, T.M. (2004) *Imagining the Nation in Nature: Landscape Preservation and German Identity, 1885–1945*. Cambridge, MA: Harvard University Press, p. 210.

2 Mosley, S. (2001) *The Chimney of the World: A History of Smoke Pollution in Victorian and Edwardian Manchester*. Cambridge: White Horse Press, pp. 45, 185.

3 Freestone, R. (1987) ' "The New Idea": The Garden City as an Urban Environmental Ideal, 1910–1930,' *Journal of the Royal Australian Historical Society*, 73, pp. 94–108, 98.

4 Longstaff-Gowan, T. (2001) *The London Town Garden, 1740–1840*. New Haven, CT: Yale University Press for the Paul Mellon Centre for Studies in British Art, p. 247.

5 Lowe, P. and J. Goyder. (1983) *Environmental Groups in Politics*. London: George Allen & Unwin, pp. 20–21.

6 Simmons, I.G. (2001) *The Environmental History of Great Britain: From 10,000 Years Ago to the Present*. Edinburgh: Edinburgh University Press, p. 225.

7 Taylor, H. (1997) *A Claim on the Countryside: A History of the British Outdoor Movement*. Edinburgh: Keele University Press, p. 32.

8 Colpita, G. (2002) *Game in the Garden: A Human History of Wildlife in Western Canada to 1940*. Vancouver, B.C., p. 71.

9 Sandlos, J. (2001) 'From the Outside Looking In: Aesthetic, Politics, and Wildlife Conservation in the Canadian North,' *Environmental History*, 6, p. 8.

10 Dunlap, T.R. (1999) *Nature and the English Diaspora: Environment and History in the US, Canada, Australia, and New Zealand*. Cambridge: Cambridge University Press, p. 195.

11 Star, P. (2002) 'Native Forest and the Rise of Preservation in New Zealand (1903–1913),' *Environment and History*, 8, p. 285.

12 Dominick, III, R.H. (1992) *The Environmental Movement in Germany: Prophets and Pioneers, 1871–1971*. Bloomington, IN: Indiana University Press, pp. 55, 61, 88.

13 Lekan, T.M. (2004) *Imagining the Nation in Nature: Landscape Preservation and German Identity, 1885–1945*. Cambridge, MA: Harvard University Press, pp. 208, 221.

14 Weiner, D.R. (1988) *Models of Nature: Ecology, Conservation, and Cultural Revolution in Soviet Russia*. Bloomington, IN: Indiana University Press, pp. 62, 135, 137, 147, 169, 170.

15 Nash, R.F. (2001) *Wilderness and the American Mind*, 4th edn New Haven, CT: Yale University Press, p. 151.

16 Turner, J.M. (2002) 'From Woodcraft to "Leave No Trace": Wilderness, Consumerism, and Environmentalism in Twentieth-Century America,' *Environmental History*, 7, p. 464.

17 Whited, T.L. (2000) *Forests and Peasant Politics in Modern France*. New Haven, CT: Yale University Press, p. 72.

18 Dunlap, T.R. (1988) *Saving America's Wildlife*. Princeton, NJ: Princeton University Press, p. 15.

19 Colpita, G. (2002) *Game in the Garden: A Human History of Wildlife in Western Canada to 1940*. Vancouver, B.C., p. 87.

20 Jacoby, K. (1997) 'Class and Environmental History: Lessons from "The War in the Adirondacks," ' *Environmental History*, 2, p. 335.

21 Olwig, K. (1984) *Nature's Ideological Landscape: A Literary and Geographic Perspective on its Development and Preservation on Denmark's Jutland Heath*. London: George Allen & Unwin, pp. 86, 87.

22 Pincetl, S. (1993) 'Some Origins of French Environmentalism: An Exploration,' *Forest & Conservation History* 37, p. 85.

23 Hutton, D. and L. Connors. (1999) *A History of the Australian Environment Movement*. Cambridge: Cambridge University Press, p. 76.

24 Nash, R.F. (2001) *Wilderness and the American Mind*, 4th edn New Haven, CT: Yale University Press, p. 115.

25 Nash, R.F. (2001) *Wilderness and the American Mind*, 4th edn New Haven, CT: Yale University Press, p. 84.

26 Krutch, J.W., ed. (1962) *Thoreau: Walden and Other Writings*. New
    York, NY: Bantam, pp. 177, 207.

27 Nash, R.F. (2001) *Wilderness and the American Mind*, 4th edn New
    Haven, CT: Yale University Press, pp. 126, 128.

28 Fox, S. (1981) *The American Conservation Movement: John Muir and His
    Legacy*. Madison, WI: University of Wisconsin Press, p. 116.

29 Moore-Colyer, R.J. (1999) 'From Great Wen to Toad Hall: Aspects
    of the Urban-Rural Divide in Inter-War Britain,' *Rural History* 10,
    p. 115.

30 Fox, S. (1981) *The American Conservation Movement: John Muir and His
    Legacy*. Madison, WI: University of Wisconsin Press, p. 12.

31 Pawson, E. (2002) 'The Meaning of Mountains,' in E. Pawson and
    T. Brooking (eds.), *Environmental Histories of New Zealand*. Victoria,
    Australia: Oxford University Press, p. 148.

32 Star, P. (2002) 'Native Forest and the Rise of Preservation in New
    Zealand (1903–1913),' *Environment and History*, 8, p. 283.

33 Gates, B.T. (1998) *Kindred Nature: Victorian and Edwardian Women
    Embrace the Living World*. Chicago, IL: University of Chicago Press,
    pp. 231–2.

34 Dunlap, T.R. (1999) *Nature and the English Diaspora: Environment and
    History in the US, Canada, Australia, and New Zealand*. Cambridge:
    Cambridge University Press, p. 108.

35 Lutts, R.H. (1998) 'The Wild Animal Story: Animals and Ideas,'
    in R. Lutts (ed.), *The Wild Animal Story*. Philadelphia, PA: Temple
    University Press, p. 3.

36 Schmitt, P.J. (1990) *Back to Nature: The Arcadian Myth in Urban
    America*. Baltimore, MD: The Johns Hopkins University Press,
    pp. 47, 49.

37 Dunlap, T.R. (1999) *Nature and the English Diaspora: Environment and
    History in the US, Canada, Australia, and New Zealand*. Cambridge:
    Cambridge University Press, p. 106.

38 Rothfels, N. (2002) *Savages and Beasts: The Birth of the Modern Zoo*. Baltimore, MD: The Johns Hopkins University Press, pp. 23–4.

39 Barrow, M.V. (2002) 'Science, Sentiment, and the Specter of Extinction: Reconsidering Birds of Prey during America's Interwar Years,' *Environmental History*, 7, p. 75.

40 Dunlap, T.R. (1999) *Nature and the English Diaspora: Environment and History in the US, Canada, Australia, and New Zealand*. Cambridge: Cambridge University Press, p. 193.

41 Price, J. (1999) *Flight Maps: Adventures with Nature in Modern America*. New York, NY: Basic Books, pp. 82, 89.

42 Kuzma, J. (2003) 'New Zealand Landscape and Literature, 1890–1925,' *Environment and History*, 9, p. 459.

CHAPTER 3

The friendly wild of post-war affluence

J.R.R. TOLKIEN, a city-dwelling intellectual, described himself in 1957 as 'a Hobbit,' who liked 'gardens, trees and unmechanized farmlands' and 'good plain food.'[1] Tolkien's fictional hobbits inhabited the rural, pre-modern world of his trilogy, *The Lord of the Rings*, that was on its way to becoming one of the most beloved stories in western literature.

The Lord of the Rings is an adventure story featuring a struggle between good and evil, and there is never any doubt which side nature is on. The admirable creatures of Middle Earth live simply and naturally. The unassuming, pre-industrial hobbits reside close to the earth. The elves understand horses and trees. The lands in which they lived are beautiful, even enchanted.

The forces of evil are surrounded by filth and darkness. In Mordor, Sauron's lair, 'nothing lived, not even the leprous growths that feed on rottenness. The gasping pools were choked with ash and crawling muds, sickly white and grey, as if the mountains had vomited the filth of their entrails upon the lands about.'[2] The cackling, ill-tempered Orcs take delight in destroying nature. They cut down trees for the fun of it and leave a sort of slime in their wake. Like Sauron, they are devoted to consuming the earth's plants and minerals to create monstrosities, death-dealing creatures and machines. Sauron's apocalyptic hatred of green, living things prompts even ancient trees (Ents) to bestir and uproot themselves to thwart him.

> *Tolkien also complained of modern, industrial life outside of his fiction. He lamented the arrival of atomic weapons, the mechanization of warfare*

Tolkien also complained of modern, industrial life outside of his fiction. He lamented the arrival of atomic weapons, the mechanization of warfare. In 1952 he lamented the traffic around Oxford: 'This charming house has become uninhabitable – unsleepable-in, unworkable-in, rocked, racked with noise, and drenched with fumes. Such is modern life. Mordor in our midst.'[3]

The Lord of the Rings enjoyed only modest success in the 1950s. Most expressions of nature loving in the two decades following World War II lacked Tolkien's harsh, anti-modern edge and were more likely to utilize than criticize technology.

Yet in the prosperous US, especially, expressions of affinity for nature grew. Nature loving occurred very much on human terms, on manicured suburban lawns, in comfortable campers, and with beloved pets. Even as scientists began to argue that nature was more chaotic and less predictable than had been imagined, millions constructed a friendly wild that complemented, not challenged, the substantial material comforts that unprecedented numbers of them enjoyed.

The threat of nuclear annihilation hung over the world like a Damocles Sword, and the anti-nuclear movement constituted the most potent challenge to the status quo between 1945 and 1960 in the US. The National Committee for a Sane Nuclear Policy in 1957 urged an end to nuclear testing and called for Americans and others to set aside nationalism in the interests of survival: 'The sovereignty of the human community comes before all others.'[4]

But most Americans expressed anxiety over nuclear war more obliquely, through exposure to popular films, novels, and songs rather than participation in protest movements. Movies such as *The Blob, Attack of the Crab Monsters, It*, and *Them* described the fearsome, monstrous mutants created by nuclear radiation.

Americans had nothing but praise for the four-wheeled monsters that were consuming so much of their time, money, and land. The automobile seemed to open up a world of pastoral possibilities. A driver early in the twentieth century found driving along Lake Michigan made the world 'everlasting, and unbelievable . . . Being in it was beyond understanding, it was incomprehensible joy.' By the 1950s the roads were bigger, the automobiles much faster and numerous, the roadside businesses ubiquitous and monotonous. Novelist John Steinbeck groused that it soon would 'be possible to drive from New York to California without seeing a single thing.'[5] But more and more Americans were taking to the road to find nature. A survey of vacationers in Colorado, the heart of the

> *Novelist John Steinbeck groused that it soon would 'be possible to drive from New York to California without seeing a single thing'*

West, found that six in ten planned to picnic, four in ten to fish, camp, or hike. The number of people camping in Illinois increased more than five-fold from 1949 to 1957. National, state, and local parks blossomed after World War II, and many featured space for a parking spot, picnic table, fire pit, and spot of ground where the new, lightweight and waterproof nylon tents could be erected and inhabited for a week or a day. Portable stoves, folding chairs constructed of aluminium and nylon, and a host of other inventions made getting away from it all easier than ever before, even as a rising proportion of campers lived more comfortably while camping than their grandparents had at home. This was especially true of the growing number of Americans who purchased trailers that could be pulled behind their automobiles. Electrified and plumbed campers featured not only beds, but also refrigerators, ovens, and toilets. Vacationers enjoyed nature through the mediation of sophisticated techno-logy, particularly automobiles.

Suburbs brought millions of Americans closer to nature in their everyday lives. Interstate highways and other new roads provided rapid, convenient access to jobs. Bulldozers, plywood, and wall-board simplified building, driving down prices and making single-standing homes available to a much wider swath of the population. Nearby strip malls offered a panoply of consumer goods – but were tucked out of sight of residences. Indeed, the genius of the suburb lay in suggesting a simple, pastoral life far removed from commerce and industry even as it more fully embraced the comforts of modern capitalism. Residents enjoyed a stable and comfortable climate year round through the intensive use of energy-gobbling technology. Solar power was discussed, then discarded, in favour of oil and natural gas. Air conditioners, invented during the Depression, increased from 43,000 in 1947 to more than one million just six years later.

Trees and lawns quickly materialized where bulldozers had so recently tread. Large lots and curvilinear 'roads' or 'lanes' (developers believed that the word 'street' connoted urbanism) added to the sense of being in a park-like, rural setting.[6] Indeed, the

Large lots and curvilinear 'roads' or 'lanes' (developers believed that the word 'street' connoted urbanism) added to the sense of being in a park-like, rural setting

amount of public land reserved for community parks shrank. New York City set aside 27 per cent of areas developed from 1900 to 1940 for parks, less than 3 per cent for post-war developments. 'Every house will have its own "park" when all the trees are grown,' explained an advertisement.[7]

The tending of lawns became, as the title of one history puts it, an 'American Obsession' after World War II.[8] The first mechanical mowers had appeared in the 1860s, but by 1900 only a very small proportion of the nation's homes featured a carefully maintained lawn. Most people could not afford the substantial time and equipment to keep them up, and, in any event, needed that space for vegetable gardens or forage for cattle, horses, or goats. Indeed, cast-iron deer appeared on the lawns of the well-to-do, as if to signify that the owners were wealthy enough to turn their property into a sort of park land – though the era's leading landscape architects found such accoutrements gauche. Lawns grew in number and extent early in the century before multiplying after World War II. New types

Suburbanization

When people walked to work, prosperous urban residents lived in or near the centre of cities. Horse and especially electric-powered forms of public transit changed this pattern in the nineteenth century, and the automobile brought much more mobility in the twentieth century, allowing people to live far away from where they worked and shopped. By the 1950s, more people lived around than inside many large cities.

Suburbanization has always offered the prospect of a closer relationship with nature. Large plots allowed for extensive yards, gardens, and trees. Unlike urban streets, dotted with businesses, suburban neighbourhoods were just for homes. This separation from the world of industry and commerce gave the park-like suburbs a feel that was natural as well as prosperous. Suburbs offered a refuge from the very modern forces that made them possible.

of grass seed, fertilizers, pesticides, and herbicides made it easier than before to maintain an attractive lawn, a single species of grass. Gasoline-powered push mowers had appeared shortly before the war and were now widely available. Riding mowers soon replaced them in many garages. Americans had purchased about thirty-five thousand lawnmowers a year in the 1930s. In 1951 they bought well over one million.

Environmentalists since Rachel Carson have been at pains to explain the costs of conventional lawns. These green seas have devoured massive amounts of water and noxious chemicals. But, like urban planners who favour high-density housing, such nay-sayers have made little impression on most Americans. Suburbanization and the sylvan landscapes that accompanied it have represented both material success and an affinity for the natural world, the trees, flowers, shrubs, and neat lawns that have surrounded these new, spacious, and beloved homes.

Working-class suburbs were, of course, less expansive, and here nature loving took a peculiar twist. Unable, through lack of space and money, to create the park-like grounds favoured by well-to-do counterparts, Americans of more modest means often populated their lawns with all manner of plastic animals and plants, from toadstools to pink flamingos, ornaments which suggested that the yard's owners could afford some conspicuous, if tasteless, consumption of their own.

A wide swath of post-war American society celebrated the domestication of nature. *Reader's Digest*, which had nearly 15 million subscribers around the world by 1950, consistently depicted a friendly wild. This emblem of middle America of course spilled a great deal of ink on

> Reader's Digest, *which had nearly 15 million subscribers around the world by 1950, consistently depicted a friendly wild*

'man's best friend,' faithful dogs that insisted on loving and serving their masters. But it also claimed that wild animals were dogs at heart. 'The Friendly Wild' was a regular column with protagonists such as the 'White Lady,' a bat that shared caresses with a man; Svea, 'The Moose Who Liked People;' and a stick-fetching fox that 'confided' to the author that 'he'd like to be a dog.' Contributors described a peccary that acted 'like a kitten,' a caribou that 'trotted behind me like a dog,' a goose that became 'as sociable as a collie pup,' an eagle that followed a man 'like a puppy.'[9]

Guns were out of place in the friendly wild. Several authors recalled the moment of epiphany when they realized that they could not shoot creatures that 'were practically human.'

But *Reader's Digest* was no hotbed of vegetarianism and animal-rights activists. The people who blanched at the thought of shooting animals had no qualms about eating them. The few articles describing farm animals indicated that these creatures were happy to sacrifice their lives for human comfort. Indeed, a piece describing laboratory animals being slowly starved to death championed 'man and animal joining together' to improve people's lives.[10]

The only animals censured by *Readers' Digest* in the 1950s were those that damaged the interests of humans. Tree-destroying bark-beetles were 'hungry gangster[s],' the screwworm fly that preyed on farm animals was 'vicious,' and the sea lamprey, which harmed commercial fisheries, was 'an evil marine vampire,' a 'monster.'[11]

These malicious animals were the exception that proved the rule. The great majority of pets, wild animals, and farm animals were friends to humanity, were familiar and beloved creatures eager to serve people.

The metamorphosis of Lassie perhaps best illustrates Americans' determination to depict animals as being obsessed with people's welfare. The collie first appeared in a *Saturday Evening Post* short story in 1938 written by Erik Knight, an Englishman who had emigrated to the US. A book, *Lassie Come Home*, followed in 1940.

Knight's Lassie is a product of canine rather than human impulses. True, she generates a tremendous sense of pride and devotion in her young owner, who credits her return with restoring harmony to his family, and her trek from Scotland constituted an impressive feat of endurance. Yet Knight attributes this accomplishment to good breeding and instinct, an innate sense of home and habit, not to squishy emotions like loyalty and love.

The long-running US television version of Lassie, which began in 1954, presented a very different sort of dog. In these stories the loyal and perceptive collie worried over and saved her family and others from calamity. This dog was no mere creature of instinct. She loved and protected her people.

Nothing did more to popularize the anthropomorphism of animals than Walt Disney's films, and none of their many films did a better job of it than *Bambi*. As with so many Disney productions, the film took considerable liberties with the book on which it was based. Hungarian Sigmund

> *No one did more to popularize the anthropomorphism of animals than Walt Disney's films, and none of their many films did a better job of it than* Bambi

Salzmann had published *Bambi: A Forest Life*, in 1926, and the novel was soon translated into English. Salzmann (whose pen name was Felix Salten) depicted a forest suffused by death. Young Bambi witnesses the killings of a mouse, a baby hare, a fox, and a squirrel which, when wounded by a ferret, 'raised his forepaws desperately and clutched his head in terror and agony while the red blood oozed on his white chest.' The Disney version, which appeared in 1942, excised these parts of the book. 'There's nobody swooping down and eating someone else,' remarked the film's story editor.[12] Disney's *Bambi* depicts a pristine forest populated by good-hearted and co-operative animals that happily co-exist without having to hunt each other. Winter brings hardship, but nature is good, and spring comes without owls feeling compelled to eat mice.

There are killers in the forest, but they are not animals. Bambi first learns that the world is not safe when his mother tells him to be cautious about entering a meadow. When shots resound the pair flee. 'Man was in the forest,' his mother explains. She does not survive her next brush with hunters, and it is left to his father to offer an explanation: 'Your mother can't be with you any more.'

The hunters return, their arrival heralded by dark, cackling birds, and we learn that these insatiable killers are the opposite of all that is natural and good. They do not seem to be the least bit interested in food. They readily shoot everything that moves, all the lovable animals that we have been prompted to care about, and they loose ravenous dogs and fire upon the forest. Bambi and his mate, Feline, escape, but the moral of the film is clear enough: humans are evil, relentless, destroyers of innocent nature.

Other Disney nature films depicted a world of amiable animals in which humans were absent. The 'True Life Adventure' series ran from 1948 to 1960, beginning with *Seal Island* and closing with *Jungle Cat*. These shows were the most complete nature documentaries to yet appear, as camera operators laboured for months to capture arresting footage of animals in their natural habitat. These animals did not talk, and they seldom – on screen, at least – interacted with humans. But the films took considerable liberties with biology. Disney observed that a pair of courting tortoises depicted in the *Living Desert* looked 'like knights in armour, old knights in battle' and decreed that the film should underscore this parallel with 'a music cue, a tongue-in-cheek fanfare.' Reviewers decried the studio's 'disposition to edit and arrange . . . so that it appears the wild life . . . is behaving in human and civilized ways.' One critic observed that these nature films patronized animals by 'summoning us to see how very nicely the humble creatures do, considering that they lack our sophistication and know-how'.[13] 'True Life' animals were at once exotic and familiar, wild and domesticated.

Disney films, like *Reader's Digest*, often stressed animals' service to people. *Old Yeller*, released in 1957 and based on a novel by Fred Gipson, features a dog that shows up on a Texas homestead in the late 1860s to stand in for the head of the house, who has left to sell some cattle. Old Yeller at first does more harm than good by driving a mule and its plough into a fence. But he never turns down a chance to risk his life to protect his family and faces down a bear, some pigs, and a wolf. This last act of heroism leaves him with rabies. Travis, the eldest son who has become utterly devoted to his pet, must now kill him. Old Yeller becomes a sort of Jesus, who willingly sacrifices his life to save his family – and brings young Travis into a deeper and more profound understanding of life. 'I'm mighty proud of how my boy stood up to it,' says his father, upon returning. 'Couldn't ask no more of a grown man.' This accomplishment, Travis's coming of age, is made possible by Old Yeller's gift of his life and death.

The nature constructed by Disney and *Reader's Digest* was actively interested in human welfare. Like suburban backyards, it was a highly domesticated extension of the suburban house

> The animals depicted by
> Reader's Digest *and*
> *Walt Disney liked people,*
> *and people liked them*

itself, whose air conditioning and central heating had transformed life into comfortable predictability. Nature had become less autonomous, less threatening. The animals depicted by *Reader's Digest* and Walt Disney liked people, and people liked them. The hunters in *Bambi*, to be sure, were anything but kind. But few viewers felt implicated in their sins. They never appear on screen, and the great majority of Disney's audience no longer killed animals in any event and were therefore amenable to treating those who did as scapegoats, as cruel, avaricious murderers too thick-headed to understand that hunting created widows and orphans. Films like *Bambi* made animals beloved and familiar. In people's beliefs and imaginations, animals became thoroughly familiar, lost their agency, the capacity to follow their own scripts, to have a life beyond the pale of human understanding. Like Tolkien's hobbits, animal kingdoms had become a sort of paradise lost, a simple, virtuous society free from machinery, aggression, greed, the features and anxieties of modern life.

This search for meaning and simplicity coloured more faithful representations of nature. Sally Carrighar, the survivor of a wretched childhood and troubled adulthood, decided to live in Sequoia National Park and to observe the animals around a large outcropping. The book which in 1944 emerged from this experience, *One Day on Beetle Rock*, seldom engaged in explicit anthropomorphism. Much like her contemporary, Rachel Carson, Carrighar made good biology accessible and interesting. Her actors are driven by instinct and largely concerned with food and safety. But behind the scenes, in researching and writing this book, Carrighar described herself as befriending these animals. She learned to share her food with them, to talk to them sincerely, with warmth. When a goshawk killed a grouse, the animals she had been observing rushed into her cabin for safety. The animals stayed for some days, and Carrighar realized that she had found 'home at last – and with these delightful children.'[14] In Carrighar's books, as in Carson's, readers were left with the impression of an orderly, harmonious world.

The emerging field of ecology in some respects validated this Edenic perspective. Frederic Edward Clements dominated the field for most of the first half of the twentieth century, and Clements emphasized the climax community. Weather and other stable geographic variables created distinctive and stable plant communities. These communities could, of course, change suddenly. Fire constituted an obvious example. But, left alone and given time, they would, through the process of succession, eventually produce a predictable and durable ecosystem. This ecosystem was 'an organism' whose diverse elements supported and interacted with each other predictably and harmoniously. J. Arthur Thompson, a Scottish biologist, referred to it as the 'web of life.'

Thinking of plants, animals, and other elements of the physical environment as a single organism or ecosystem had obvious practical ramifications. It called into question modern humans' tendency to favour some parts

> *Thinking of plants, animals, and other elements of the physical environment as a single organism or ecosystem had obvious practical ramifications*

Sally Carrighar, 1898–1985

Many nature lovers have found in the outdoors or animals a sense of peace, harmony, or even love that eluded them in human relations. This was certainly true of Sally Carrighar, whose autobiography is aptly entitled *Home to the Wilderness*.

The first child of a comfortable Cleveland couple, she was plagued by ill health. Her mother's hatred harmed her much more. She turned to animals for solace. At the age of twelve she befriended a chipmunk in the park. Her mother accused her of meeting a man there. A dog joined her in her walks between school and home, and she literally found her voice in talking with him. Her mother ordered her to 'get rid of that dog.' 'You have to learn not to love,' she explained.[15]

Adulthood brought a reprieve from such cruelty, but not happiness. Carrighar attended college, then became a production secretary in Hollywood and wrote for magazines, advertisers, and radio. Hungry and despondent during the Depression, she considered suicide before seeking therapy with a skilled analyst who helped her come to terms with her harrowing childhood. But she still had not settled on how to make a living.

Then, in her sorrow, she heard the little birds outside her window. She began leaving seeds for them, and one day a tattered, one-legged linnet, named the Brave Lass by Carrighar, came inside. She and the birds had begun to understand each other. One night she heard a delicate voice accompanying the classical music on her radio. It was a mouse! Carrighar realized her calling: to become a nature writer. 'My whole future life burst open that night,' she later recalled, 'like some great and beautiful flower.'[16]

Carrighar's first book, *One Day on Beetle Rock*, described her careful observations in Sequoia National Park. She went on to other wilderness homes in the Grand Tetons and the Arctic, places that she described in loving detail for the rest of us.

over others. Ecologists therefore began to argue that predators ought to be allowed to live because they formed an essential and unique function within an ecosystem. 'I dislike no animal because he eats,' remarked one.[17]

The emerging field of ecology provided scientific grounds for criticizing utilitarian foresters and fish and wildlife biologists who treated pine trees, cod, and deer like rows of turnips to be harvested at rates determined by static mathematical formulae. Ecologists argued that sustained human intervention in ecosystems was bound to alter and often degrade a given landscape, that pollution, exotic species, and other human-induced disruptions brought profound, often unpredictable changes. Modern humanity disrupted and degraded complex but stable ecosystems.

Ecology

This scientific field of study arose early in the twentieth century and emphasized the relationship between elements of an environment that had been studied or approached discretely. Ecologists argued that a forest, for example, should be understood as a complex organism whose various parts – plants, mammals, insects, soils, bacteria – acted in concert with and relation to each other.

Ecology became a more recognizable field in the years after World War II, and by the 1960s many environmentalists were using it to justify setting aside wilderness areas where nature would be allowed to maintain its natural balance, free from human interference. But ecologists were by then debating the premise that any such balance existed and raising the question of whether humans should be considered part of or alien to ecosystems.

But more nuanced ecologists were pointing out that even 'natural' ecosystems were much more dynamic than they seemed. Herbert Gleason and A.G. Tansley, of the US and England, respectively, suggested before World War II that plants succeeded each other in capricious ways and that human interventions in such communities were not necessarily harmful. Post-war ecologists followed them in depicting even ecosystems outside direct human influence as indeterminate and unpredictable. One could draw up a model of how a patch or field free from human incursions would become a climax forest in one thousand years. But only a small fraction of such places would, in fact, remain free from unanticipated, perhaps catastrophic, events during that time: fires, wind storms, or climate shifts, for example. Nature, it turned out, was not particularly stable. 'We are foundering on the rocks of complexity,' wrote one ecologist.[18]

This sort of complexity did not much influence the writings of Aldo Leopold, who emerged as the most popular ecologist in the US after World War II. *A Sand County Almanac*, the rambling and eloquent book he was working on when he died in 1948, tried to get people to take the requirements and rights of nature more seriously. 'We abuse land because we regard it as a commodity belonging to us,' he explained. 'When we see it as a community to which we belong, we may begin to use it with love and respect.'[19] He advocated a 'land ethic' in which people shifted their role from 'conqueror of the land-community to plain member and citizen of it.' This required an end to narrow economic and utilitarian thinking. 'A thing is right when it tends to preserve the integrity, stability, and beauty of the biotic community,' he asserted. 'It is wrong when it tends otherwise.'[20]

Aldo Leopold, 1887–1948

Leopold was an important and influential ecologist of the mid-twentieth century both because of the content of his ideas and his knack for conveying them to a much broader audience than most scientists reached.

Leopold's parents planted a red oak to commemorate his birth, and the boy spent much of his childhood in the Iowa woods, often shooting and observing birds. By the age of fifteen he was keeping an ornithology journal, and he went off to study in Yale University's new forestry programme. Having graduated in 1909, he joined the Forest Service and headed for New Mexico.

Leopold's parents planted a red oak to commemorate his birth, and the boy spent much of his childhood in the Iowa woods, often shooting and observing birds

Despite obdurate health problems, Leopold became an influential conservationist in the Southwest. By 1914 he was urging his peers and supervisors to concern themselves with more than grazing permits; the Forest Service ought to create game reserves for endangered animals, a plan that, with enthusiastic support from hunters, bore fruit. By the 1920s Leopold's brand of conservation had broadened to include soil erosion and wilderness preservation. 'Of what avail are forty freedoms without a blank spot on the map?' he asked.[21] True, wolves killed cattle and game animals, creatures that humans prized. But ecology, the young field that Leopold took an interest in, suggested that wolves and fire played a crucial role in keeping deer and forests, respectively, healthy. Moreover, Leopold remained haunted by the 'fierce green fire' that had died in the eyes of a wolf he had shot in the Southwest.[22] Perhaps such a creature had an inalienable right to life.

Leopold did not advocate these ideas quietly. He wrote and spoke and worked with a variety of interest groups to change how the Forest Service did business. He received *Outdoor Life's* gold medal for conservation in 1931, and his *Game Management* was at last published in 1933.

This book cemented Leopold's national reputation and landed him a position heading the University of Wisconsin's graduate programme in game management, the first in the nation, and he joined President Roosevelt's Committee on Wild Life Restoration.

Leopold's ideas became less orthodox after he became an academic. *A Sand County Almanac*, published in 1949, foreshadowed the development of deep ecology in the 1970s and remains the most beloved text of many contemporary environmentalists. It stands as the most enduring legacy of a very influential and active man.

Yet increasing numbers of Leopold's colleagues were not so sure that nature was inherently stable, a sort of Eden that could be preserved or restored, and of course beauty was in the eye of the beholder. Some ecologists offered a rationale for preservation. Others questioned the premises that lay behind it.

Ecology still had a low public profile in the western world in the fifteen years following World War II, a period when the environmental movement grew slowly – if at all. Moving to the suburbs and tending one's lawn and garden prompted little concern over the bulldozing of ecosystems. Camping and other forms of outdoor recreation did not elicit criticism of the

Ecology still had a low public profile in the western world in the fifteen years following World War II, a period when the environmental movement grew slowly – if at all

automobile culture that made parks and wild areas so much more accessible. Watching films and reading stories about friendly and lovable wild animals that created harmonious communities did not spawn an animal-rights movement. As the 1960s opened, western people in general and Americans in particular found no contradiction in celebrating and subduing nature, in simultaneously seeking nature and a growing standard of living.

But the long-standing, if seldom acknowledged, tension between enjoying prosperity and nature was about to attract a great deal of attention.

Recommended reading

Meredith Veldman's *Fantasy, the Bomb, and the Greening of Britain: Romantic Protest, 1945–1980* (Cambridge: Cambridge University Press, 1994) includes a fascinating interpretation of Tolkien and some other fine material on romanticism and nature loving. Strong studies of post-war nature-loving in the US include: Virginia Scott Jenkins, *The Lawn: A History of an American Obsession* (Washington, DC: Smithsonian Institution Press, 1994); Adam Rome, *The Bulldozer in the Countryside: Suburban Sprawl and the Rise of American Environmentalism* (Cambridge: Cambridge University Press, 2001); David Ingram, *Green Screen: Environmentalism and Hollywood Cinema* (Exeter: University of Exeter Press, 2001); Roderick Frazier Nash, *The Rights of Nature: A History of Environmental Ethics* (Madison, WI: University of Wisconsin Press, 1989). Leopold is treated in James I. McClintock, *Nature's Kindred Spirits: Aldo Leopold, Joseph Wood Krutch, Edward Abbey, Annie Dillard, and Gary Snyder* (Madison, WI: University of Wisconsin Press, 1994).

Notes

1   Veldman, M. (1994) *Fantasy, the Bomb, and the Greening of Britain: Romantic Protest, 1945–1980*. Cambridge: Cambridge University Press, p. 79.

2   Veldman, M. (1994) *Fantasy, the Bomb, and the Greening of Britain: Romantic Protest, 1945–1980*. Cambridge: Cambridge University Press, p. 82.

3   Veldman, M. (1994) *Fantasy, the Bomb, and the Greening of Britain: Romantic Protest, 1945–1980*. Cambridge: Cambridge University Press, p. 87.

4   Brands, H.W. (1993) *The Devil We Knew: Americans and the Cold War*. New York: Oxford University Press, p. 63.

5   Jakle, J.A. (1985) *The Tourist: Travel in Twentieth-Century North America*. Lincoln, NB: University of Nebraska Press, pp. 65, 190.

6   Jackson, K.T. (1985) *Crabgrass Frontier: The Suburbanization of the US*. New York, NY: Oxford University Press, p. 236.

7   Rome, A. (2001) *The Bulldozer in the Countryside: Suburban Sprawl and the Rise of American Environmentalism*. Cambridge: Cambridge University Press, p. 122.

8   Jenkins, V.S. (1994) *The Lawn: A History of an American Obsession*. Washington, DC: Smithsonian Institution Press.

9   Peterson del Mar, D. (1998) ' "Our Animal Friends": Depictions of Animals in *Reader's Digest* during the 1950s,' *Environmental History*, 3, pp. 30–1.

10 Peterson del Mar, D. (1998) ' "Our Animal Friends": Depictions of Animals in *Reader's Digest* during the 1950s,' *Environmental History*, 3, pp. 32, 35.

11 Peterson del Mar, D. (1998) ' "Our Animal Friends": Depictions of Animals in *Reader's Digest* during the 1950s,' *Environmental History*, 3, p. 33.

12 Cartmill, M. (1993) *A View to Death in the Morning: Hunting and Nature through History*. Cambridge, MA: Harvard University Press, pp. 163, 171.

13 Schickel, R. (1968) *The Disney Version: The Life, Times, Art and Commerce of Walt Disney*. New York, NY: Simon and Schuster, pp. 288–90.

14 Carrighar, S. (1973) *Home to the Wilderness*. Boston, MA: Houghton Mifflin, p. 330.

15 Carrighar, S. (1973) *Home to the Wilderness*. Boston, MA: Houghton Mifflin, p. 84.

16 Carrighar, S. (1973) *Home to the Wilderness*. Boston, MA: Houghton Mifflin, p. 275.

17 Nash, R.F. (1989) *The Rights of Nature: A History of Environmental Ethics*. Madison, WI: University of Wisconsin Press, pp. 56–8.

18 Barbour, M.G. (1995) 'Ecological Fragmentation in the Fifties,' in W. Cronon (ed.), *Uncommon Ground: Rethinking the Human Place in Nature*. New York, NY: W.W. Norton, p. 247.

19 Nash, R.F. (1989) *The Rights of Nature: A History of Environmental Ethics*. Madison, WI: University of Wisconsin Press, p. 69.

20 Leopold, A. (1970) *A Sand County Almanac, with Essays on Conservation from Round River*. San Francisco, CA: Sierra Club and New York, NY: Ballantine, pp. 240, 262.

21 Nash, R.F. (2001) *Wilderness and the American Mind*, 4th edn New Haven, CT: Yale University Press, p. 189.

22 Nash, R.F. (1989) *The Rights of Nature: A History of Environmental Ethics*. Madison, WI: University of Wisconsin Press, p. 64.

CHAPTER 4

Nature and counter-culture

JACK KEROUAC'S *Dharma Bums*, a 1958 novel, proved to be prophetic in questioning prosperity and conformity while touting an expansive individualism. Like Thoreau before him, he believed that a higher, more conscious self was to be forged in nature, away from the artificialities of the modern world. Kerouac urged his readers to travel and live simply in wild areas, to instigate 'a great rucksack revolution' of 'thousands or even millions of young Americans wandering around with rucksacks, going up to mountains to pray . . . giving visions of eternal freedom to everybody and to all living creatures.'[1]

In the 1960s and early 1970s, western people embraced the wild and the natural with much more enthusiasm than ever before. Nature loving cut a wide swath in these years, captivating strident students, beatific hippies, John Denver fans, or the millions of television viewers who delighted in the *Undersea World of Jacques Cousteau*. By the mid-1970s, a reverence for the wild and the natural resided at the heart of western culture.

The 1960s brought unprecedented prosperity to most of Europe. In the Netherlands just 8 per cent of households had a car in 1957,

The 1960s brought unprecedented prosperity to most of Europe

4 per cent a television. A decade later those numbers had risen to 45 and 80 per cent, respectively. Most citizens of France and Italy lacked the household appliances that were proliferating in the US in the years following Word War II. But even working-class and rural couples were apt to own an automobile, radio, washing machine, refrigerator, and a gas stove by the late 1960s. Parisians' expenditures on consumer goods rose nearly twenty-fold between 1949 and 1974. Just 10 per cent of French people indicated no sense of deprivation of material goods in 1957. In 1969 that percentage had risen to 35. West Europeans by then enjoyed synthetic clothes, frozen food, and a wide array of plastics. They were also much more likely to live in cities. Agriculture, forestry, or fishing occupied 42 per cent of Italian workers in 1951, just 17 per cent two decades later.

Americans had been enjoying the fruits of prosperity before Europeans did, but their comforts also expanded in the 1960s. The proportion who enjoyed some sort of air conditioning tripled during the decade, for example.

As before, prosperity spawned a backlash against itself, a search for deeper meanings beyond the bounds of modernity and technology. Many of 'the rainbow colours of the culture of the sixties were painted on the fragile bubble of a despised affluence, an economic boom that was simply taken for granted.'[2]

The universities that young people flocked to became breeding grounds for alienation and dissent. These children of the growing middle class were accustomed to being heard and taken seriously. Now, in their late teens, they ran smack into implacable and impersonal institutions indifferent to their sensibilities, opinions, and desires. The number of university students in Britain multiplied from 50,000 before the war to more than 200,000 by the late 1960s. In West Germany, too, higher education grew dramatically, as the government struggled to meet

Student movement

The student movement arose across the western world in the 1960s on burgeoning university and college campuses. Here young people who had grown up free from the concerns of war or poverty confronted large, impersonal institutions that seemed unresponsive to their individuality and concerns.

Many students soon turned their attentions to developments beyond their campuses: war, imperialism, capitalism, and, in the US, the civil rights movement

Many students soon turned their attentions to developments beyond their campuses: war, imperialism, capitalism, and, in the US, the civil rights movement. Many were drawn to various environmental movements, as the protection of nature implied a critique of both the older generation and the status quo. But environmental concerns were seldom at the centre of radical university organizations.

The student movement – always more diffuse than focused – faded in the late 1960s and early 1970s, though it had by then nurtured a generation of moderate and radical reformers, and university campuses would remain a fertile ground for groups concerned with improving society.

the economy's demand for a more knowledgeable workforce. But university culture remained decidedly pre-modern and hierarchical, government funding inadequate to meet the new, ambitious goals. Students therefore found themselves paying more and more for anachronistic courses in unresponsive institutions.

The ensuing protests that convulsed western campuses in the late 1960s were seldom about the environment *per se*. Students from Berkeley to Berlin demanded more control over university decisions, an end to imperialism, and class revolution.

But a deep distrust of modern, mechanistic society underlay these diverse protests. 'No to the consumer society!' shouted students at the Sorbonne in 1968.[3]

Youthful dissenters soon split into two camps, particularly in the US. Political activists, by definition, sought to change the way their world was structured, sought to reform government policies or to overturn government itself. They wanted to create Black Studies departments, to compel France and the US to withdraw from Algiers and Vietnam, respectively. More alienated youth lacked the optimism or dedication of their militant counterparts. They sought fulfilment through individual acts of pleasure and meaning.

Cultural or life-style radicals commonly embraced the natural, non-human world as an alternative to the drab conformity of modern life. They had 'a semiconscious concept of almost mystical union with nature, with their own inner lives, or with other people.'[4] Drugs such as marijuana or LSD commonly fuelled this sense of fusion and transcendence, as did frequent and uninhibited sexual encounters.

Observers commonly referred to hippies as 'flower children,' an appellation that, in the words of Arthur Marwick, 'expressed the beautiful essence of nature and the exact opposite of the plastic.' Flowers were sometimes used to make more particular political statements, as when anti-war protestors gently placed them in the barrels of guns. But they more commonly signified the achievement of a more amorphous, inner sort of peace that depended not on changing the minds of warmongers but on deciding to live more authentically, more naturally. 'If you're going to San Francisco, be sure to wear some flowers in your hair,' crooned Scott Mackenzie.[5] Thousands of young people followed this advice literally, and parts of that city were soon full of young, long-haired men and women seeking their peculiar version of the good life.

> *Other hippies took to the countryside. Here, as one advocate of rural communalism put it, one could return 'to the primal source of consciousness, the true basis of culture: the land'*

Other hippies took to the countryside. Here, as one advocate of rural communalism put it, one could return 'to the primal source of consciousness, the true basis of culture: the land'.[6] Northern New Mexico had become a hub for such movements by the late 1960s. Captain America of *Easy Rider*, the classic 1969 film, celebrates living on the land: 'You do your own thing in your own time.'[7] A sixteen-year-old making himself at home in Yosemite National Park explained: 'There are no real values left in society. We come here because it is beautiful, it is real.'[8]

Nature served as the unifying force in 'Woodstock,' Joni Mitchell's anthem for the counter-culture. 'A child of God . . .

walking along the road' was 'gonna camp on the land/ And try and get my soul free.' Bombers 'were turning into butterflies above our nation.' The chorus: 'We are stardust, we are golden/ And we've got to get ourselves back to the garden.'

More conventional thinkers were also embracing the wild. The Faith-Man-Nature Group of the US began working with the National Council of Churches in the mid-1960s and linked theologians with scientists. The World Council of Churches began holding regular conferences on the environment in the 1970s, and the Presbyterian Church and American Lutheran Church officially expressed concern over the state of the environment early in that decade. Western Christians had long asserted a

---

Counter-culture

The counter-culture blossomed in the mid-1960s, as growing numbers of young people rejected the verities of growth and conformity that had long resided at the centre of western civilization. Although nurturing radical political movements attacking capitalism, imperialism, and racism, the counter-cultural movement was often apolitical. Closely related to the spread of hallucinogenic drugs, it could focus more on altering people's consciousnesses than political structures.

Affinity for nature resided at the heart of the counter-cultural movement: beards, long hair, flowers, living close to if not off the land. Many of the counter-culture's symbols could be appropriated without much changing one's standard of living, and one of the movement's many ironies was the ease with which advertisers commandeered its images and slogans to hawk their wares. But if the counter-cultural movement did not slow western nations' consumption of the environment, it multiplied the number of people who expressed an affinity for and concern for it.

right to use the earth as they saw fit. Now many were urging each other to reconsider humans' relationship with the rest of the world.

> *Non-Christian thinkers embraced environmentalism with a religious, even apocalyptic faith*

Non-Christian thinkers embraced environmentalism with a religious, even apocalyptic faith. Alan Watts, once an Episcopal priest, turned to Zen Buddhism and by the late 1950s was arguing in widely read books that people were part of, not separate from, nature.

Charles Reich, in a book tellingly entitled *The Greening of America*, prophesied that the coming revolution would create 'a renewed relationship of man to himself, to other men, to society, to nature, and to the land.' This revolution was necessary to rescue the nation from the tyranny of technology and environmental destruction, developments he associated with both the disappearance of community and the 'loss of self.' 'Of all the changes that have happened to man,' he concluded, 'perhaps the deepest and least understood is his loss of the land, of weather, of growing things, and of the knowledge of his body that these things give.' The various cultural and social movements devoted to re-establishing a deeper connection with one's environment, one's friends, and oneself were therefore monumental developments. 'For one who thought the world was irretrievably encased in metal and plastic and sterile stone,' Reich concludes, 'it seems a veritable greening of America.'[9]

Theodore Roszak's *The Making of a Counter-Culture: Reflections on the Technocratic Society and Its Youthful Opposition* also deprecated the scientific consciousness for 'progressively estranging us from the magic of the environment.' 'The strange youngsters who don cowbells and primitive talismans and who take to the public parks or wilderness to improvise outlandish communal ceremonies' were therefore revitalizing democracy.[10]

More than three decades later, blessed with hindsight, it is difficult to read Reich and Roszak without laughing out loud. The hippie movement proved to be more flash than substance. It made little headway outside the US, where some 200,000 young men and women out of a population of 300 million dropped out of school, jobs, and other encumbrances to seek inner bliss. Most of these people soon pursued more conventional lives. Indeed, the parachute of prosperity so certain that one could take it for granted made 'dropping out' possible and desirable. 'It is only after technology has triumphed, and only for those whose lives are glutted with the goodies it provides, that some of the youth can begin to look nostalgically back at the delights of shamanism.'[11]

Nor was the nation's corporate culture shy about appropriating people's growing affinity for the wild and free and turning it towards consumption. Everyone from cereal makers to automobile manufacturers to record executives were literally capitalizing on America's new-found love of 'nature.'

Movements, practices, and gestures that began as protests of mass, technological society had a habit of circling back around to the very sort of values their founders had derided. Technological

> *Movements, practices, and gestures that began as protests of mass, technological society had a habit of circling back around to the very sort of values their founders had derided*

advances, fibreglass and Styrofoam made surfboards much lighter and surfing more popular in the 1950s in California, Hawai'i, and Australia. But the elemental nature of the pastime, the blending of young, tanned bodies, crashing surf, and expansive beaches, soon made it a symbol of nonconformity and self-expression among young men with increased leisure time on their hands. 'The surfers are the new noble savages,' remarked an historian in 1974.[12] One Australian devotee termed it 'the ultimate liberating factor on the planet.'[13] Recreation had become a political act. 'By simply surfing,' asserted a believer in 1970, 'we are supporting the revolution.'[14] But surfing, like rock music, was by then more a part of corporate and consumer society than an alternative to it, and although some described it as 'working with nature,' the titles of Australian books asserted a domineering ethos: *Surf: Australians Against the Sea* and *Gladiators of the Surf*.[15] More people than ever before were finding meaning in the outdoors, through camping, hiking, surfing, downhill and water skiing, boating, and skin or scuba diving. But although these activities represented an increased affinity for nature, they hardly constituted the sort of counter-cultural 'greening,' the renunciation of technology and materialism, that Reich had prophesied.

A yearning for simpler times ran deep in the popular culture of the 1960s and 1970s. *National Geographic*, which had long featured peoples and places deemed primitive and exotic to western readers, increased its circulation more than five-fold from 1957 to 1971, to over seven million. England's Jane Goodall, who had lovingly put earth worms under her pillow as a two-year-old, flouted scientific protocol in her studies of chimpanzees in Africa by cultivating personal relationships with her subjects. One day, when she offered a chimp she had named David Graybeard a nut, he 'gently held my hand' to acknowledge her kindness. 'We had communicated in a language far more ancient than words, a language that we shared with our prehistoric ancestor, a language bridging our two worlds.'[16] Goodall found an audience eager for these stories of connection across this divide in her books, articles in *National Geographic*, speeches, and television appearances. This was also the time when J.R.R. Tolkien's *The Lord of the Rings* trilogy, which lovingly depicted the beauty and triumph of pre-modern sensibilities and landscapes, became an international bestseller.

Another British writer, Richard Adams, captivated millions of western readers with his tale of virtuous creatures searching for home in a chaotic, mechanized world. *Watership Down*, published in 1972 after a succession of rejections, chronicled

> *British writer, Richard Adams, captivated millions of western readers with his tale of virtuous creatures searching for home in a chaotic, mechanized world*

the struggle of a group of independent rabbits to establish their own warren. Like Tolkien's hobbits, Adams's rabbits were threatened by the forces of industrial progress. One group, influenced by Fiver's premonition of disaster, fled their homes shortly after the appearance of a sign announcing the planned development of 'HIGH CLASS MODERN RESIDENCES.' Only a few of the remaining rabbits escaped the poisoning and shooting that ensued, which was followed by a bulldozer that 'tore the field to bits.' 'Men will never rest till they've spoiled the earth and destroyed the animals,' explained one.[17] (Life imitated art inasmuch as the profits from *Watership Down* allowed Adams to escape his job as a government bureaucrat.)

This same distrust of modern humanity and society suffuses the work of Farley Mowat, the widely read Canadian writer.

Mowat's first book, *People of the Deer*, depicted Eskimos' struggle to survive in the face of bureaucratic indifference. Mowat also used animals as a foil to critique modern Canadian society. In *The Dog Who Wouldn't Be*, condensed by *Reader's Digest*, he celebrated the life of his boyhood dog, the beloved and mischievous Mutt. Mutt's death at the hands of irresponsible modernity (in the form of a careening truck) 'made an end to the best years that I had lived,' pushing Mowat 'into the darkening tunnel of the years.'[18]

The themes explored in *The Dog Who Wouldn't Be* are more patent in *Never Cry Wolf*, a popular book published in 1963 that eventually became a Disney movie. The story recounts Mowat's work for the Canadian Wildlife Service, when he claimed to discover that wolves subsisted largely on mice and maintained a reciprocal rather than predatory relationship with caribou by hunting diseased rather than healthy animals.

But the biology of *Never Cry Wolf* was more romantic than scientific. Mowat became a sort of wolf. He adjusted his sleep and diet to mirror the animals he was studying. He marked his territory by urinating. His admiration for the wolves grew apace. He hoped to some day meet a woman as attractive as 'Angeline,' the female wolf of the den he was near. He peppered his prose with unflattering (to humans) comparisons between wolves and people. 'The wolf never kills for fun,' he remarked, 'which is probably one of the main differences distinguishing him from man.' He had found no evidence of wolves ever taking

> *'The wolf never kills for fun,' he remarked, 'which is probably one of the main differences distinguishing him from man'*

a human life in northern Canada, 'although there must have been times when the temptation [due less to hunger than to human cruelty and obtuseness] was well-nigh irresistible.'

That Mowat could not really join their society signified the tragedy of the human condition, the inability to re-enter 'the lost world which once was ours before we chose the alien role' of modern life.[19]

The gulf between human and animal had grown still wider by the time Mowat wrote *A Whale for the Killing* a decade later, in 1972. He and his wife then lived in a remote part of Newfoundland, among elderly, independent-minded neighbours whom he was glad to report had no use for the 'poor bloody bastards' who were '*grateful* for the chance to work for de owner in dat stinkin' shithole [the local factory] down to t'Reach for de rest of dere lives, so's dey can buy some goddamn t'ing.' So far, so good: Mowat and his many readers could be counted on to agree with this indictment of modern life.

But local opinion turned against Mowat and his sensibilities when he used his celebrity to defend a Fin Whale that became stranded in a local lake. As in *Never Cry Wolf*, Mowat thought more highly of the whale than of most of his fellow humans. The trapped animal was noble and long suffering, meek and mild. He approvingly quoted an elderly fisherman who described whales as likely being 'the smartest creatures in God's ocean . . . and maybe out of it as well.' But the locals, whom he had admired 'as a natural people, living in at least some degree of harmony with the natural world,' seemed 'nauseatingly anxious to renounce all that and throw themselves into the stinking quagmire of our society which has perverted everything natural within itself, and is now busy destroying everything natural outside itself.' Residents shot the whale, which soon died from these wounds. Mowat wept, and 'not just for the whale that died, but because the fragile link between her race and mine was severed' yet again.[20]

More mainstream nature lovers produced less melancholy treatments of their subject. Jacques Cousteau began to capture international attention with his stunning underwater photography in the 1956 film, *The Silent World*. A decade later his *Undersea World of Jacques Cousteau* captured unprecedented numbers of television viewers. The shows were a pot-pourri of instruction and entertainment, 'a slice of aquatic life with the dull bits cut out,' as one biographer put it.[21] In 'Octopus, Octopus,' for example, Cousteau hoped to generate understanding and sympathy for these much maligned animals. But he prompted two octopuses to fight for the camera by pushing them together, nearly killing one. The film also featured a local diver and marine biologist described by Cousteau as 'well rounded, quite striking in a bathing suit . . . A James Bond heroine.' Much of the show was devoted to shots of her brushing her long hair.[22]

Environmentalists and scientists alike criticized Cousteau for being a huckster more interested in spectacle and self-promotion than in conservation or knowledge. A French critic said that he bore the same relation to oceanography as the 'French cancan . . . to *Swan Lake*.'[23]

But Cousteau realized that nature, individualism, and adventure were tightly braided in the western mind.

Jacques Cousteau, 1910–97

Cousteau was born to indulgent and comfortable parents. An indifferent student but curious child, he was fascinated by water at an early age. He served in the French Navy and took up underwater diving in the 1930s to find 'my eyes opened to the world beneath the surface of the sea.'[24] He soon began a long preoccupation with devising masks, snorkels, oxygen tanks – any paraphernalia that might allow him to go more deeply into the ocean's depths. He developed an aqualung during the war that broke the ten-metre barrier and facilitated the clearing of mines.

Cousteau purchased a former mine sweeper, dubbed it the 'Calypso,' and began perfecting underwater film making. He wrote *The Silent World*, the first of many books on what lay beneath the ocean's surface, and it sold well. But it was his Oscar-winning documentary film of the same title released in 1956 that made Cousteau famous.

Cousteau's timing was apt. For crew he could draw from a growing population of 'sensitive young men who had not found happiness or peace in leading an ordinary life.' He also found an audience feeling much the same way eager to explore with him from their living rooms. He signed a $4.2 million contract with ABC television to film a series of twelve hour-long shows. *The Undersea World of Jacques Cousteau* would, in fact, run for nearly nine years and reach audiences of forty million, more than any other documentary series ever had.

Cousteau thought of himself as a rationalist, a man who believed that humans could use both nature and technology to improve the human prospect. But he also saw nature, particularly the ocean, as a place of adventure.

> *Cousteau thought of himself as a rationalist, a man who believed that humans could use both nature and technology to improve the human prospect*

Cousteau used his influence to advocate many types of preservation and conservation. He testified to the US Congress about oceanic pollution and over fishing. The Cousteau Society, which he founded in 1974, promoted research, education, and conservation.

So did John Denver, a folksinger who much admired Cousteau. There was nothing subtle about Denver's appeal. He sang 'about the mountains, the wilderness, about love and family.' Many found his offerings saccharine and shallow. Ensconced in his beloved Colorado mountains, he dismissed critics as 'people working in big cities, on big newspapers or magazines.'[25] His anthem, 'Rocky Mountain High', took a swipe at developers: 'Why they try and tear the mountains down/ To

---

John Denver, 1943–97

Born Henry John Deutschendorf, Jr., Denver's childhood was a caricature of American rootlessness, as his father dragged the family from one military base to another. Young John often felt awkward and out of place. He once gave a party to which no one came. Like so many shy children before him, Deutschendorf turned to nature for solace. 'The out-of-doors was my first and truest best friend,' he later recalled.[26] He moved to Los Angeles in 1964, where he struggled to succeed as a singer and songwriter and changed his name to 'Denver.' Success finally came in 1971, with the recording of 'Country Roads.' This was followed by 'Rocky Mountain High' and a string of other hits which made Denver the most popular songwriter in the world.

Denver worked hard to live up to the ideals expressed in his songs. Two divorces and an enthusiasm for drugs tarnished his wholesome image. But he cultivated an interest in meditation, yoga, and eastern religion, collaborated with humanitarians as diverse as Jacques Cousteau and President Jimmy Carter, and was the first major western artist of his day to tour the Soviet Union and China. He shovelled millions of dollars into Windstar, an organization devoted to improving the environment.

Denver died in an aircraft accident at the age of fifty-three, long after his public profile had receded.

---

bring in a couple more, more people, more scars upon the land.' But, like Denver's other hits, this was no protest song. 'Rocky Mountain High' was a paean to the beautiful place where Denver felt he belonged: 'Coming home to a place he's never been before,' to 'starlight,' 'silver clouds,' 'the forests and the streams,' a 'clear blue mountain lake,' and soaring eagles. His music conjured up a vision of 'America before the fall.'[27]

Denver claimed to be 'more effective in achieving the revolutionary goal of transforming the collective conscience of the world in what I do than politicians are.' A *New York Times* review of a performance disagreed: 'An ecologist and a strip miner would have been able to leave Mr Denver's concert with equally clear consciences.'[28] Like so much of nature loving, Denver's music had more to do with salving the wounds inflicted by an increasingly anonymous, mechanized society than with transforming that society.

> *Denver claimed to be 'more effective in achieving the revolutionary goal of transforming the collective conscience of the world in what I do than politicians are'*

Like Denver, Cousteau's popularity was ultimately rooted in a widely shared, transcendent vision. Impatient with the strictures of governments, marriage, old age, and conventional religion, Cousteau advocated the unfettered pursuit of 'instincts, needs, pleasures, drives' and desired 'to play without measuring the consequences.' The aquatic world that he introduced millions of people to seemed to hold out that promise. We are drawn to him, a biographer concludes, 'because he embodies that yearning we have to live by our impulses.'[29]

Nature constituted the counter-culture's alternative to conformity and sterility. It symbolized freedom.

Prosperous people's romantic attachments to nature were nothing new. The 1960s and early 1970s differed from previous era in the breadth and depth of that affinity for nature. But they also constituted a departure in the extent to which western citizens were willing and determined to undertake political battles on nature's behalf.

Recommended reading

Protest movements are addressed in: Arthur Marwick, *The Sixties: Cultural Revolution in Britain, France, Italy, and the US, c. 1958–c. 1974* (Oxford: Oxford University Press, 1998); Kenneth Keniston, *Youth and Dissent: The Rise of a New Opposition* (New York, NY: Harcourt Brace Jovanovich, 1971). Strong treatments of individuals include: Alex Lucas, *Farley Mowat* (Toronto: McClelland and Stewart, 1976); Axel Madsen, *Cousteau: An Unauthorized Biography* (New York, NY: Beauford Books, 1986); Richard Munson, *Cousteau: The Captain and His World* (New York, NY: William Morrow, 1989); John Collis, *John Denver: Mother Nature's Son* (Edinburgh: Mainstream Publishing, 1999; Sy Montgomery, *Walking with the Great Apes: Jane Goodall, Dian Fossey, Biruté Galdikas* (Boston, MA: Houghton Mifflin, 1991).

Notes

1 Tamney, J.B. (1992) *American Society in the Buddhist Mirror*. New York, NY: Garland, p. 65.

2 Dickstein, M. (1977) *Gates of Eden: American Culture in the Sixties*. New York, NY: Basic, p. 210.

3   Keniston, K. (1971) *Youth and Dissent: The Rise of a New Opposition*.
    New York, NY: Harcourt Brace Jovanovich, p. 313.

4   Keniston, K. (1971) *Youth and Dissent: The Rise of a New Opposition*.
    New York, NY: Harcourt Brace Jovanovich, p. 239.

5   Marwick, A. (1998) *The Sixties: Cultural Revolution in Britain, France,
    Italy, and the US, c. 1958–c. 1974*. Oxford: Oxford University Press,
    p. 483.

6   Rudnick, L.P. (1996) *Utopian vistas: The Mabel Dodge Luhan House and
    the American Counterculture*. Albuquerque, NM: University of New
    Mexico Press, p. 218.

7   Ingram, D. (2001) *Green Screen: Environmentalism and Hollywood
    Cinema*. Exeter: University of Exeter Press, p. 145.

8   Stucker, G. (1971) 'Youth, Rebellion & the Environment,'
    Environmental Journal, April, p. 8.

9   Reich, C.A. (1970) *The Greening of America*. New York, NY: Random
    House, pp. 4, 9, 173, 395.

10 Roszak, T. (1969) *The Making of a Counter-Culture: Reflections on the
    Technocratic Society and Its Youthful Opposition*. Garden City, NY:
    Doubleday, pp. 252, 265.

11 Keniston, K. (1971) *Youth and Dissent: The Rise of a New Opposition*.
    New York, NY: Harcourt Brace Jovanovich, pp. 341–2.

12 Howell, S. (1974) *The Seaside*. London: Studio Vista, p. 199.

13 Booth, D. (1995) 'Ambiguities in Pleasure and Discipline: The
    Development of Competitive Surfing,' *Journal of Sport History*, 22,
    p. 196.

14 Booth, D. (2003) 'Expression Sessions: Surfing, Style, and Prestige,'
    in R.E. Rinehard and S. Sydnor (eds.), *To the Extreme: Alternative
    Sports, Inside and Out*. Albany, NY: State University of New York
    Press, p. 319.

15 Booth, D. (1995) 'Ambiguities in Pleasure and Discipline: The
    Development of Competitive Surfing,' *Journal of Sport History*, 22,
    pp. 194, 196.

16 Goodall, J., with P. Berman. (1999) *Reason for Hope: A Spiritual Journey*. New York, NY: Warner, p. 81.

17 Adams, R. (1972) *Watership Down*. New York, NY: Macmillan, pp. 7, 136, 140.

18 Mowat, F. (1957) *The Dog Who Wouldn't Be*. Boston, MA: Atlantic Monthly Press, p. 238.

19 Mowat, F. (1963) *Never Cry Wolf*. Boston, MA: Little, Brown, pp. 203, 228, 246.

20 Mowat, F. (1972) *A Whale for the Killing*. Boston, MA: Atlantic Monthly Press, pp. 33, 43, 147, 223.

21 Madsen, A. (1986) *Cousteau: An Unauthorized Biography*. New York, NY: Beaufort Books, p. 153.

22 Munson, R. (1989) *Cousteau: The Captain and His World*. New York, NY: William Morrow, p. 136.

23 Madsen, A. (1986) *Cousteau: An Unauthorized Biography*. New York, NY: Beaufort Books, p. 227.

24 Madsen, A. (1986) *Cousteau: An Unauthorized Biography*. New York, NY: Beaufort Books, p. 22.

25 Collis, J. (1999) *John Denver: Mother Nature's Son*. Edinburgh: Mainstream, 1999, p. 15.

26 Collis, J. (1999) *John Denver: Mother Nature's Son*. Edinburgh: Mainstream, 1999, p. 33.

27 Collis, J. (1999) *John Denver: Mother Nature's Son*. Edinburgh: Mainstream, 1999, p. 15.

28 Collis, J. (1999) *John Denver: Mother Nature's Son*. Edinburgh: Mainstream, 1999, p. 102.

29 Munson, R. (1989) *Cousteau: The Captain and His World*. New York, NY: William Morrow, pp. 249, 252.

CHAPTER 5

Breakthrough

THE SCENE: A FICTIONAL 'town in the heart of America where all life seemed to live in harmony with its surroundings,' a place replete with fine farms and orchards, foxes, deer, birds, clear, trout-filled streams. 'Then a strange blight crept over the area and everything began to change.' Livestock died. Fish expired. Trees and shrubs browned and withered. Children sickened, then died. The birds stopped singing. The town confronted a 'silent spring.'

Eden had been defiled, and Rachel Carson pointed her finger at the snakes. After depicting the death throes of ground squirrels poisoned by insecticides, she wonders 'who among us,' who among the millions of Americans and others who mutely tolerated the wanton killing of innocent creatures, was not 'diminished as a human being?' Could any people, she wondered rhetorically, 'wage relentless war on life without destroying itself, and without losing the right to be called civilized.'[1]

most of the people enjoying comfortable homes and automobiles lacked a first-hand, everyday acquaintance with wringing their food or their livelihood from nature

Carson's *Silent Spring* ignited the green fire of environmentalism and the western world was ready to hear her eloquent message. The number of prosperous people had increased dramatically since World War II, and most of the people enjoying comfortable homes and automobiles lacked a first-hand, everyday acquaintance with wringing their food or their livelihood from nature. Millions of young people took prosperity for granted and questioned the verities and platitudes of their elders, tendencies that primed them to question the necessity of war, industrial capitalism, and environmental exploitation. Never before had people with so much been uneasy over so much.

The match that ignited this tinder in 1962 was struck by an unlikely actor. Rachel Carson, a reclusive, middle-aged writer and biologist from the eastern US was close to death when *Silent Spring* appeared that year. Yet her book galvanized people – and not a few governments – to change substantially the way in which they understood and interacted with nature.

Carson, like the heart of the environmental movement she galvanized, was more moderate than radical. She had a faith in human reason and science, and the movement she inspired reformed, not transformed, modern, industrial uses of nature. In an era of extreme, even utopian, blueprints for reworking western life, environmental reform tended to be moderate and pragmatic.

Silent Spring drew a great deal of attention. The chemical industry, accustomed to being congratulated for fostering agricultural prosperity and eradicating malaria, felt the sting of Carson's arrows and spent a quarter of a million dollars depicting Carson as a 'hysterical fool'.[2] But President Kennedy cited the book approvingly, and a 1963 Presidential Scientific Advisory Committee validated her charges. More to the point, perhaps, the book sold more than half a million copies in hardback alone and soon spread to many other nations. Her voice was not alone. *Our Synthetic Environment* by the intellectual, Murray Bookchin (whose pen name was Lewis Herber), and *The Quiet Crisis* by politician Stewart Udall appeared about the same time. But Carson's voice was by far the clearest and most compelling.

Silent Spring depicted environmental degradation as insidious, a cancer that weakened ecosystems and animals for years or even decades before people awoke to its presence. But patent environmental catastrophes appeared in the book's wake. The sewage in the Great Lakes became so noxious that a popular magazine deemed Lake Erie 'a North American Dead Sea.'[3] More than one million people signed a petition to save it. In 1966 a pile of coal sludge in Wales washed over and killed 144 people. Soon after, the tanker *Torrey Canyon* spilled many tons of crude oil on Britain's beaches. Three years later an accident off the coast of California resulted in a similar disaster, and a river in Cleveland caught fire. Toxic wastes poisoned tens of thousands of birds along those shores and Germany's Rhine. Birds and beaches coated with tarry oil made for great television, as millions of viewers across the globe watched innocent animals suffering and dying because of human folly. Carson's prophesies were bearing putrid fruit in the western world's living rooms.

Rachel Carson, 1907–64

Like many other children born early in the twentieth century, Rachel Carson soon took an interest in birds and other animals. She criticized her older brother for hunting rabbits. At Pennsylvania College for women she majored in English, then biology, and after a summer at the ocean in 1929 she went to graduate school at Johns Hopkins, where she studied marine zoology and received a master's degree.

Carson soon combined her passions for nature and writing. She began working as a biologist for the federal government in 1935 and in 1937 published an article on the ocean in the *Atlantic Monthly*. Her first book, *Under the Sea Wind*, appeared four years later. Her big break came in 1949, when she won a fellowship that funded work on *The Sea Around Us*, which became a bestseller, was translated into thirty-three languages, and made Carson famous. *The Edge of the Sea* followed in 1955 and was also very well received.

> *Carson strove to convey the ways in which various elements of an ocean's ecosystem interacted with each other, knowledge that she gleaned from long hours of painstaking observation*

Up to this point, Carson's work was a judicious blend of compelling prose and good, engaging science. Carson strove to convey the ways in which various elements of an ocean's ecosystem interacted with each other, knowledge that she gleaned from long hours of painstaking observation and more conventional academic research. The oceanic world depicted in these widely read books was beautiful, balanced, and, ultimately, vulnerable. Humans could destroy its equilibrium. Carson combined, as one biographer puts it, 'a child's sense of wonder . . . and an abiding sense of responsibility.'[4] But nature's beauty, not people's destructiveness, lay at the heart of Carson's first three books.

Long interested in the pesticide DDT, Carson was worried about its impact on the environment in the late 1950s. Being diagnosed with cancer in 1957 may have made her sensitive to unseen but powerful threats to the world's health. Or perhaps she simply decided to express herself more boldly in what would in all likelihood be her last book. In any event, *Silent Spring* would combine the grace and scientific detail of Carson's earlier offerings with a patent and urgent anger that stimulated millions of readers to take a keen interest in the environment and its degradation.

The growing concern for the environment had legs, particularly in the US. 'We were just sitting here,' recalled a member of the National Wildlife Federation, 'and suddenly there they were, knocking at the doors.'[5] That organization had over 500,000 members by 1970. The Sierra Club had 113,000, up from 20,000 in 1959.

The growing concern for the environment had legs, particularly in the US. 'We were just sitting here,' recalled a member of the National Wildlife Federation, 'and suddenly there they were, knocking at the doors'

These sorts of numbers gave environmental organizations unprecedented political clout. The trend had begun in 1956, when the Sierra Club and Wilderness Society succeeded in stopping a dam on the Colorado River. Never before had the preservation of wilderness so soundly trumped economic development. Emboldened by victory, environmentalists proposed an ambitious national wilderness system encompassing about 2 per cent of the nation's land. The bill met stiff resistance. But thousands of citizens wrote letters to Congress supporting it, and a more moderate version passed easily in 1964. Plans to build dams in the Grand Canyon prompted full-page advertisements by the Sierra Club in *The New York Times* and *The Washington Post* and prompted what a senator called 'one of the largest letter-writing campaigns which I have seen.' In 1967 Secretary of the Interior Udall announced that the Johnson administration had changed its mind. 'Hell has no fury like a conservationist aroused,' observed a congressman. Congress in 1968 passed legislation instituting the National Wild and Scenic Rivers System to ensure that some rivers, at least, would be preserved 'in their free-flowing condition.'[6]

Sierra Club

Founded in 1892 and headed for many years by John Muir, the Sierra Club was for several decades the principal advocate of large parks in the US. It emerged as a potent political force in the 1950s, when it successfully opposed a dam in Dinosaur National Monument and began urging that millions of acres of land be set aside for wilderness, an unprecedented effort that bore fruit in the Wilderness Act of 1964. It then led efforts, again successful, to stop the damming of the Grand Canyon.

By the 1970s the Sierra Club had been joined and in some respects eclipsed by more radical environmental groups. But through its Legal Defense Fund and lobbying activities, and supported by hundreds of thousands of members, it remains one of the most influential and well-funded environmental organizations in North America.

Concern over pollution and other broad environmental problems also grew. Los Angeles had begun cleaning its air after World War II by targeting both industrial sources and private garbage incinerators. But its resolution was unusual. This changed in the 1960s. Congress passed the Clean Water, Clean Air, and Solid Waste Acts between 1960 and 1965, and subsequent legislation soon stiffened their provisions. A welter of additional laws followed. The impact of suburban development on wetlands and floodplains elicited criticism, then regulation. Dolphins killed in the taking of tuna were protected, many toxic pesticides and herbicides were banned, and much, much more. Two pieces of legislation were particularly important. The Environmental Protection Agency, established in 1970 and soon staffed with several thousand employees, was charged with enforcing environmental laws, particularly the identification and rehabilitation of toxic waste sites. The Endangered Species Act of 1973 put the preservation of threatened species ahead of economic development.

'Ecology,' observed one politician, had 'become the political substitute for motherhood,' and Richard Nixon, the president liberals loved to hate, was astute enough to recognize it.[7] Three months before Earth Day, Nixon called for 'reparations for the damage we have done to our air, to our land and to our water.'[8] He arguably passed the most substantial set of environmental laws of any president in the

'Ecology,' observed one politician, had 'become the political substitute for motherhood,' and Richard Nixon, the president liberals loved to hate, was astute enough to recognize it

nation's history and even went so far as to call for an end to the poisoning of predators on private land and to more closely regulate lead-based paints. Critics, then and later, asserted that Nixon was opportunistic, even cynical, that appropriating the least threatening component of the counter-cultural and protest movements served to contain and isolate their radical cores. Nixon in fact identified the environment as the nation's 'common cause,' a way for its strife-ridden people to move 'beyond factions.'[9] The degree to which a Republican president proved willing to regulate free enterprise testifies to the depth and breadth of environmentalism's political power in the US in the years around 1970.

Environmental sensibility peaked in the US with the first Earth Day, a phenomenon that exhibited both the potential and the limitations of the movement. Appearing in 1970, just when mainstream Americans felt whipsawed by violence and extremism at home and abroad, Earth Day was self-consciously wholesome and moderate. One of the event's organizers, a young, radical law student, later explained that he and other planners 'didn't want to alienate the middle class; we didn't want to lose the "silent majority" just because of style issues.'[10] Nearly all of the Earth Day gatherings were therefore more celebratory than political. The federal government and several corporations, including Dow Chemical, provided funding. Leftist naysayers not surprisingly dismissed Earth Day as an attempt to use 'rock and roll, idealism and non-inflammatory social issues to turn the youth off from more urgent concerns which might really threaten our power structure.'[11]

The radical left was ambivalent over the emerging environmental movement. Environmental and social devastation alike

Earth Day

Conceived by US Senator Gaylord Nelson as a sort of national 'teach-in,' Earth Day drew approximately 20 million people, mostly students, across the US on April 22, 1970. Probably the biggest demonstration of its very eventful era, it was much more celebratory and less shrill than protests having to do with war or race.

Subsequent American Earth Day celebrations were smaller, though the movement spread to other countries. It remains an occasion for politicians to espouse a green agenda, environmental organizations to claim some space in the media, and nature lovers across the ideological spectrum to plant trees and learn about environmental issues.

could simply be understood as the logical end of capitalism. Yet most environmentalists seemed more interested in cleaning up around the edges of modern industrialism's excesses than in mounting a fully-fledged critique of it. Environmentalism provided a congenial home for moderates determined to curb pollution and protect selected species.

Environmentalism also flexed its muscles in western Europe from the late 1960s to the mid-1970s, though the movement was at first more modest than in the US.

Like their counterparts in Los Angeles, necessity had driven Londoners to get serious about smoke abatement in the 1950s, when authorities implicated the London Fog of December 1952 in the deaths of some 4,000 people. Greenbelts around cities, national parks, and land held by the National Trust proliferated. An anti-nuclear movement spread in the late 1950s. A 1960 demonstration in Trafalgar Square in London drew close to

> *Like their counterparts in Los Angeles, necessity had driven Londoners to get serious about smoke abatement in the 1950s, when authorities implicated the London Fog of December 1952 in the deaths of some 4,000 people*

100,000 people, and a year later the Campaign for Nuclear Disarmament had about 900 chapters. Membership in the National Trust, the venerable organization devoted to preserving places of historic interest or natural beauty, skyrocketed. The Conservation Society, concerned with broad issues such as population and economic growth, doubled its membership between 1970 and 1974. Letters to editors expressing concern over the environment increased more than twenty-fold between 1965 and 1973. A Royal Commission on Environmental Pollution appeared, and a spate of legislation followed from 1973 to 1976: the Water, Control of Pollution, Dumping at Sea, and Endangered Species Acts. 'It is a bold politician who risks' the 'disapprobation' of environmentalists, an observer noted.[12]

Britain also produced a pair of influential books in the early 1970s. *Blueprint for Survival* urged readers to recognize and

---

E.F. Schumacher, 1911–77

Born in 1911 to an economist and a mathematician, Schumacher left Germany in 1930 as a Rhodes Scholar. He lived in New York City, returned to Germany, then, in 1937, went to England, where he spent three months in an internment camp. By 1942 he had settled into a career as an economist.

By 1950 Schumacher was pursuing unconventional, non-rational ideas, from eastern religions to flying saucers to astrology. 'I feel as men during the Renaissance must have felt,' he wrote. He began to garden organically on his four acres in Surrey, an experience which convinced him 'that nature is an unbelievably complicated, self-balanced system in which the unconsidered use of partial knowledge can do more harm than good.' He concluded that 'chemical agriculture has over-reached itself. It is working against nature instead of with her.'[13]

Schumacher's spirituality found its way into his economics. A member of the National Coal Board, he began to question widely held assumptions about prosperity. The 'addiction to a purely quantitative concept of economic growth' was both spiritually bankrupt and squandered precious, non-renewable resources.[14]

Schumacher was something of a voice crying in the wilderness in the late 1950s, but the western world was ready for him by the time his *Small is Beautiful Economics as if People Mattered* in 1973. Schumacher, a Catholic, argued that Christianity and other religions required people to approach the environment, prudently and humbly. Humans' arrogance had wrought comfort, but not meaning, and the comfort was not sustainable. The West, furthermore, had imposed both poverty and socio-cultural dislocation on the Third World.

Unlike many of his peers, Schumacher was optimistic about humanity's capacity to change, to trade in unfettered capitalism's mania to 'maximise consumption' for an economics that would 'maximise human satisfaction.' As his title suggested, Schumacher favoured intermediate technologies, machinery that obviated the need for inhumane toil without depriving 'man of the kind of work that he enjoys most, creative, useful work with hands and brains.'[15] Meaning, not gross national product, counted most.

Small is Beautiful became a bestseller and brought its author twenty to thirty speaking invitations a week, including not a few offers from corporations such as Shell. He attracted audiences in the thousands on US campuses and met President Carter, before his demanding schedule led to his death less than five years after the book that made him famous had appeared.

respect the earth's limits. 'The principal defect of the industrial way of life with its ethos of expansion is that it is not sustainable,' read the first sentence of the first chapter.[16] E.F. Schumacher, in *Small is Beautiful*, was more optimistic but also called for a radical restructuring of western society and priorities, arguing that smaller-scale technologies and economies were more humane and durable.

Yet British environmentalism remained something of a top-down movement and reflected, as one scholar puts it, 'the deep cultural alienation of the British upper classes with the industrialization process.'[17] Aristocratic members of the National Trust shepherded legislation through Parliament. The government funded the Trust and other conservation-minded organizations, and leaders of these groups advised bureaucrats at the Department of the Environment. Even the Conservation Society, one of Britain's leading radical environmental groups, cautioned members to 'beware of even appearing to be associated with those who are simply agitators or protestors.'[18]

Britain's centralized, semi-private system of regulation muffled the influence of reformers

Working within the system had its costs. Government administrators consulted with the National Trust, but they continued to work most closely with industry, agriculture, and labour, powerful groups whose interests seldom intersected with those of environmentalists. Britain's centralized, semi-private system of regulation muffled the influence of reformers.

Environmentalists also met with mixed success on the continent to the mid-1970s. West Germany established a Council of

Environmental Experts in 1972 and required environmental impact assessments in 1975. But its days as an environmental leader lay in the future. It did little to regulate automobile emissions, as the industry had proved crucial to its post-war recovery. France, like Germany, had a substantial anti-nuclear movement in the 1970s. Some 15,000 rallied for that cause in a 1971 demonstration. But the movement fragmented, and France soon led the world in the proportion of electricity generated from nuclear power. French environmentalists succeeded in stopping a proposed ski resort in Vanoise National Park when half a million citizens wrote to protest about it, and a small Ministry of the Environment appeared in 1971. The Dutch, long accustomed to manipulating the land and waters of their small country, were generally optimistic about overcoming environmental problems in the late 1960s and early 1970s. The Ministry of Public Health and Environmental Hygiene, established in 1971, emphasized regulation at the 'end of the pipe.' Radicals at first articulated a broader vision. Around 1970 counter-cultural groups such as the 'Gnomes' began focusing on healthy air and water. A leftist environmental movement also emerged in Denmark. In 1969 the annual seminar of the University of Copenhagen's natural history society was disrupted by some twenty students who locked themselves in the room, shut off its ventilation, burned garbage, and doused a wild duck in oil. 'Come on and save it,' they screamed at the elder conservationists. 'You talk about pollution. Why don't you do something about it?.'[19] But Danish environmental groups soon became more practical and pragmatic, especially as the government, which had been committed to growth at any cost, integrated environmental concerns into its policies.

Sweden entered the late 1960s with a strong, centralized government that responded quickly to environmental problems. *Silent Spring* attracted many readers and helped to prompt a ban on mercury in the pulp industry in 1967. The amount of literature on environmental problems multiplied over the years. Sweden's 1968 Environmental Protection Law was probably the world's most comprehensive. When a discrete environmental movement arose late in the decade the government integrated many of its concerns.

Southern Europeans expressed much less concern over the environment in the 1960s. Italian conservationists, for example, remained focused on birds and old buildings

Southern Europeans expressed much less concern over the environment in the 1960s. Italian conservationists, for example, remained focused on birds and old buildings.

The environmental movement fared much better in Australia. Each of its states had laws addressing water and air pollution by the 1970s. As in the US, Australians were particularly concerned with protecting their wildest areas. The amount of land reserved for conservation began to grow dramatically in the late 1960s. The Little Desert Settlement plan of 1968 helped to galvanize a wilderness movement. Part of an attempt to relocate urban dwellers to Australia's extensive, largely unpopulated hinterland, the proposal alarmed those who wished the Little Desert's plants, animals, and landscape to remain undisturbed. The preservationists won.

They turned their attentions to the Great Barrier Reef. The world's largest reef had become, in the years following World War II, a popular tourist destination. By the 1960s conservationists worried over several developments: oil spills and blowouts; the prolific Crown of Thorns starfish, which was evidently consuming the reef's hard coral; and a proposed fertilizer mine on the reef. Six years of advocacy bore fruit in 1975, when the Great Barrier Reef Marine Park was born.

This early legislation emphasized multiple use, but setting aside appreciable chunks of land that could have been mined or developed nevertheless constituted a major shift in Australian priorities. An observer had complained in 1968: 'any suggestion of restraint, or request for second thoughts on some local development guaranteed to provide a quick and sure economic pay-off, is only too easily brushed aside as unrealistic or even unpatriotic.' This growth-oriented tradition was at last confronted by a potent and growing ecological sensibility. Secondary students routinely studied ecology by the early 1970s, and Premier Henry Bolt spoke favourably of 'conservation' in his 1970 election speech.[20]

A similar transformation transpired in Canada, another place whose residents had long regarded nature as more robust than fragile. In 1970 69 per cent of Canadians agreed that pollution constituted a very serious problem, and by then the federal government was passing environmental legislation. In Ontario, the nation's largest province, hunters, canoeists, and naturalists demanded in the early 1960s that more land be protected from development – and that land already set aside be preserved more fully. 'A lax and indecisive parks policy' had 'allowed many national parks to deteriorate into commercialized, honky-tonk resorts' dedicated to 'separating tourists from their money.'[21] By 1974 the Algonquin Wildlands League had succeeded in reserving large swaths of land for primitive use only. The same organization got logging stopped in a large provincial park. As in the US, Canadian biologists and ecologists began considering how broader environmental factors – including over fishing and pollution – affected the falling numbers of economically valuable fish.

The environmental quickening across the western world spawned some major international efforts

The environmental quickening across the western world spawned some major international efforts. The Partial Test Ban Treaty of 1963 reflected the concerns of many people and nations over the radioactive fallout from more than 400 detonations by the US, Soviet Union, Great Britain, and France since 1945. The International Union for the Protection of Nature was formed in 1948 to help sundry national and international preservation groups co-ordinate their activities, and it began to receive adequate funding in the mid-1950s. The United Nations, long indifferent to environmental issues, turned a corner in 1972 by sponsoring a conference in Stockholm on the Human Environment that drew more than 400 organizations and government representatives from across the globe. It paid particular attention to acid rain, a phenomenon which elicited criticism from Canada and Scandinavia of the US, Great Britain, and West Germany. The Stockholm conference also created the United Nations Environmental Programme, which would monitor and research a host of global environmental issues, despite modest funding.

A surprising amount of concern over the environment had surfaced by the mid-1970s in the Soviet Union, where strongly worded laws about people's health had always given way to economic imperatives. Environmental activism rose after Stalin's death. In 1958 students at Tartu State University and the Estonian Agricultural Academy formed the first organization devoted to nature protection. They patrolled the *druzhina,* or nature reserves, to harass poachers, a pastime that won them few friends among the hard-pressed populace or Soviet officials who winked at violations of anti-hunting regulations. A growing number of intellectuals associated preservation of nature with nationalism. 'The Russian character is impossible to imagine without' its 'expanses of forest,' asserted Vladimir Chivilikhim. 'Does the introduction of such good things as electricity and residential neighborhoods obligatorily have to be accompanied by the crushing of the flowers? Must industrial beauty *replace* natural beauty?.'[22] Like Europeans before him, Chivilikhim located the essence of his country's identity in the forests, history, and folk culture of the countryside.

This growing discomfort with unfettered change and modernization coalesced around plans to dam Lake Baikal, the largest body of fresh water in the world. 'We don't have the right to destroy the harmony and beauty of this unique gift to nature,' asserted a scientist.[23] The effort to preserve Lake Baikal failed. But the effort was historic.

The Soviet leadership particularly feared conservation movements in its satellite countries, discerning, quite correctly, that these movements expressed and fuelled nationalism. 'Folksongs, folklore, old traditions, one's own language, dialect, never die in the countryside,' remarked a Lithuanian patriot in 1971.[24]

> *The Soviet leadership particularly feared conservation movements in its satellite countries, discerning, quite correctly, that these movements expressed and fuelled nationalism*

By that year the Lithuanian Nature Protection Association had some 20,000 members, and those numbers quickly grew. One opponent of Soviet development was sent to prison camp. Others died mysteriously. Most eastern Europeans were more circumspect. Much of East Germany's environmentalism found expression in its churches, which took urban children to the countryside, planted trees, tended organic gardens, and sponsored meatless days – all under the rubric of simple living, not nationalism. But nationalism was embedded in celebrations of regional nature.

Western Europeans also used environmentalism to express nationalism. British opponents of nuclear weapons found in the bomb a symbol of technology run amuck and expressed a nostalgia for times in which life was more meaningful – and England more powerful. Hence a Campaign for Nuclear Disarmament pamphlet likened the movement to 'our finest hour in 1940.'[25] Charles de Gaulle hoped that his 'nation of 120 cheeses' could put itself at the forefront 'of scientific and technological progress . . . without France ceasing to be France.'[26]

Barely ten years after *Silent Spring's* publication, awareness of and legislation regarding the environment had increased exponentially across most of the western world. But environmental proponents and legislation seldom repudiated material and technological progress.

The Club of Rome, an international consortium of prominent scientists and intellectuals, issued its influential *The Limits to*

Growth in 1972. As its title implied, this book argued, with an overwhelming battery of statistics, that the world would reach its bursting point within a century if radical steps were not taken to create a 'sustainable state of global equilibrium.'[27]

The Limits to Growth and similar books which appeared in the 1970s signified a new chapter in the history of nature loving.

The environmental movement of the 1960s and early 1970s was broad and multifaceted. Some focused on the preservation of wilderness, others on the threats of various forms of pollution. Many western nations had powerful and influential environmental lobbies by the end of this period, others did not. But the great majority of the various movements across the western world shared a reformist orientation. Like Rachel Carson, they believed that western civilization was a very positive development, that its continuation required tempering impulses of greed and domination that threatened to consume nature and humankind alike. Preservationists sought to rescue but a tiny fraction of public land from mining and logging. The great majority of those concerned with pollution – members of environmental groups and government regulators alike – sought to mitigate and minimize the impact of industry upon people and the rest of nature, not to close these industries down.

> *The environmental movement of the 1960s and early 1970s was broad and multi-faceted. Some focused on the preservation of wilderness, others on the threats of various forms of pollution*

The Limits to Growth and other pronouncements called gradualist, reformist measures into question and began to deconstruct the intellectual assumptions that long supported western civilization and expansion. The environmental movement would soon become more extreme in its condemnation of modern society and in the solutions it proposed.

Recommended reading

Broad treatments include: John McCormick, *Reclaiming Paradise: The Global Environmental Movement* (Bloomington, IN: Indiana University Press, 1989); Anna Bramwell, *The Fading of the Greens: The Decline of Environmental Politics in the West* (New Haven, CT: Yale University Press, 1994); B.W. Clapp, *An Environmental History of Britain since the Industrial Revolution* (London: Longman, 1994); David Evans, *A History of Nature Conservation in Britain*, 2nd edn (London: Routledge, 1992); Albert Weale, *The New Politics of Pollution* (Manchester: Manchester University Press, 1992); Andrew Jamison, et al., *The Making of the New Environmental Consciousness: A Comparative Study of the Environmental Movements in Sweden, Denmark and the Netherlands* (Edinburgh: Edinburgh University Press, 1990); Robert Gottlieb, *Forcing the Spring: The Transformation of the American Environmental Movement* (Washington, DC: Island Press, 1993); Stephen Dovers, ed., *Australian Environmental History: Essays and Cases* (Melbourne: Oxford University Press, 1994). Kirkpatrick Sale's *The Green Revolution: The American Environmental Movement, 1962–1992* (New York, NY: Hill & Wang, 1993) is a concise and strong survey of its subject. Useful specialized studies include: George M. Warecki, *Protecting Ontario's Wilderness: A History of Changing Ideas and Preservation Politics, 1927–1973* (New York, NY: Peter Lang, 2000); Libby Robin, *Defending the Little Desert:*

The Rise of Ecological Consciousness in Australia (Victoria: Melbourne University Press, 1998). Mary A. McCay's *Rachel Carson* (New York, NY: Twayne, 1993) is a fine biography. Charles T. Rubin, *The Green Crusade: Rethinking the Roots of Environmentalism* (New York, NY: Free Press, 1994) includes several biographies of environmental leaders.

Notes

1 Carson, R. (1970) *Silent Spring*. New York, NY: Fawcett Crest, pp. 13, 95, 96.

2 Sale, K. (1993) *The Green Revolution: The American Environmental Movement, 1962–1992*. New York, NY: Hill and Wang, p. 4.

3 Steinberg, T. (2002) *Down to Earth: Nature's Role in American History*. New York, NY: Oxford University Press, p. 248.

4 McCay, M.A. (1993) *Rachel Carson*. New York, NY: Twayne, p. 85.

5 Sale, K. (1993) *The Green Revolution: The American Environmental Movement, 1962–1992*. New York, NY: Hill and Wang, p. 13.

6 Nash, R.F. (2001) *Wilderness and the American Mind*, 4th edn New Haven, CT: Yale University Press, pp. 230, 235, 236.

7 Dowie, M. (1995) *Losing Ground: American Environmentalism at the Close of the Twentieth Century*. Cambridge, MA: MIT Press, p. 33.

8 Gottlieb, R. (1993) *Forcing the Spring: The Transformation of the American Environmental Movement*. Washington, DC: Island Press, p. 108.

9 Dryzek, J.S., et al. (2002) 'Environmental Transformation of the State: The USA, Norway, Germany, and the UK,' *Political Studies*, 50, p. 665.

10 Gottlieb, R. (1993) *Forcing the Spring: The Transformation of the American Environmental Movement*. Washington, DC: Island Press, p. 107.

11 Dowie, M. (1995) *Losing Ground: American Environmentalism at the Close of the Twentieth Century*. Cambridge, MA: MIT Press, p. 25.

12 Vogel, D. (1986) *National Styles of Regulation: Environmental Policy in Great Britain and the US*. Ithaca, NY: Cornell University Press, p. 43.

13 Wood, B. (1984) *Alias Papa: A Life of Fritz Schumacher*. London: Jonathan Cape, pp. 230, 237.

14 Veldman, M. (1994) *Fantasy, the Bomb, and the Greening of Britain: Romantic Protest, 1945–1980*. Cambridge: Cambridge University Press, pp. 289–90.

15 Schumacher, E.F. (1975) *Small is Beautiful: Economics as if People Mattered*. New York, NY: Perennial, pp. 58, 151.

16 Goldsmith, E., et al. (1972) *Blueprint for Survival*. Boston: Houghton Mifflin, p. 3.

17 Rüdig, W. (1995) 'Between Moderation and Marginalization: Environmental Radicalism in Britain,' in B.R. Taylor (ed.), *Ecological Resistance Movements: The Global Emergence of Radical and Popular Environmentalism*. Albany, NY: State University of New York Press, p. 225.

18 Vogel, D. (1986) *National Styles of Regulation: Environmental Policy in Great Britain and the US*. Ithaca, NY: Cornell University Press, p. 52.

19 Jamison, A., et al. (1990) *The Making of the New Environmental Consciousness: A Comparative Study of the Environmental Movements in Sweden, Denmark and the Netherlands*. Edinburgh: Edinburgh University Press, p. 66.

20 Robin, R. (1998) *Defending the Little Desert: The Rise of Ecological Consciousness in Australia*. Victoria: Melbourne University Press, pp. 134, 137.

21 Warecki, G.M. (2000) *Protecting Ontario's Wilderness: A History of Changing Ideas and Preservation Politics, 1927–1973*. New York, NE: Peter Lang, pp. 117–18.

22 Weiner, D.R. (1999) *A Little Corner of Freedom: Russian Nature Protection from Stalin to Gorbachëv*. Berkeley, CA: University of California Press, pp. 335, 338.

23 Weiner, D.R. (1999) *A Little Corner of Freedom: Russian Nature Protection from Stalin to Gorbachëv*. Berkeley, CA: University of California Press, p. 357.

24 Idzalis, A. (1983) 'Institutional Response to Environmental Problems in Lithuania,' *Journal of Baltic Studies*, 14, p. 302.

25 Veldman, M. (1994) *Fantasy, the Bomb, and the Greening of Britain: Romantic Protest, 1945–1980*. Cambridge: Cambridge University Press, p. 145.

26 Bess, M. (1995) 'Ecology and Artifice: Shifting Perceptions of Nature and High Technology in Postwar France,' *Technology and Culture* 36, p. 836.

27 Meadows, D.H., et al. (1972) *The Limits to Growth: A Report for the Club of Rome Project on the Predicament of Mankind*. New York, NY: Universe Books, p. 180.

CHAPTER 6

Radical departures

LATE AT NIGHT, IN THE wild river canyon, Dr. A.K. Sarvis was cataloguing his long list of evils, including: mines, pipelines, smelters, coal-burning and nuclear power plants. He ended with 'the people who throw beer cans along the highways.'

But at this point his audience of two demurred. 'Why the fuck shouldn't I throw fucking beer cans along the fucking highway?' demanded one. 'Any road I wasn't consulted about that I don't like, I litter,' added the other. 'It's my religion.'[1]

This interchange, near the beginning of Edward Abbey's *The Monkey Wrench Gang*, neatly exhibits a new sensibility emerging by the mid-1970s, when this influential novel appeared. Earth Day and most of the environmental activism and legislation of the past decade had been about tidying up capitalism's excesses. Roadside litter was offensive because it symbolized modern people's disregard for nature's beauty. But growing numbers of environmentalists took issue with the road, not the cans, bottles, and other refuse spattered beside it. Meaningful change, they argued, entailed and required far more than cleaning up our garbage. People in the western world needed to think and to live in a radically different way.

Environmentalism had attracted moderate reformers in the 1960s. By the 1970s, as more radical movements shrivelled, concern over the environment attracted many of the West's most utopian and determined leftists.

By the 1970s, as more radical movements shrivelled, concern over the environment attracted many of the West's most utopian and determined leftists

The so-called 'doomsday' environmentalists prophesied that nothing less than a radical departure from the status quo would save the world from environmental catastrophe. Paul Ehrlich's *The Population Bomb*, published in 1968, argued just what its title implied: that overpopulation was leading humanity to the brink of a massive die-off. It quickly became the best-selling environmental book ever published, and by 1970 Ehrlich was speaking to groups of up to 10,000. In Britain the best-selling *A Blueprint for Survival*, published in 1972, warned that 'if current trends are allowed to persist, the breakdown of society and the irreversible disruption of the life-support systems on this planet, possibly by the end of the century, certainly within the lifetimes of our children, are inevitable.'[2] A spate of other books which appeared in the 1970s made the same prediction: *The Last Days of Mankind, The Death of Tomorrow, The Coming Dark Age*, among others. Humanity's very existence was imperilled.

Other radicals expressed concerns for the rest of creation. Peter Singer in 1973 proposed an addition to Black Liberation, Gay Liberation, and Women's Liberation: Animal Liberation.

A year later, in an article unsubtly entitled 'All Animals Are Equal,' he remarked: 'If a being suffers, there can be no moral justification for refusing to take that suffering into consideration.' He then catalogued the cruelties that humans subjected modern animals to, cages too small for chickens or pigs to even turn around in, the cosmetics and shampoos forced into the eyes of rabbits, the shocks administered to laboratory dogs. Unthinking consumption of meat, asserted Singer, was 'a clear instance of the sacrifice of the most important interests of other beings [a decent life – and life itself] in order to satisfy trivial interests of our own.' To stop eating meat 'may be difficult,' but it is no more difficult than it would have been for a white Southerner to go against the gradations of his society and free his slaves.'[3]

To equate eating meat with owning slaves was strong stuff and augured a radical reconfiguration of humanity's place in the cosmos. But a still less measured voice did as much or more than any other to change young people's minds and lives, especially in the US.

Edward Abbey's *Desert Solitaire* 'almost singlehandedly made it impossible for nature writing to lapse back into babbling brooks and heavenly birdsong.'[4] Abbey's 1968 book celebrated inhospitable environments, especially the deserts of Arizona, New Mexico, and Utah, landscapes that forced humans to 'confront directly the antehuman, that *other world* which frightens not through danger or hostility

> *Edward Abbey's* Desert Solitaire *'almost singlehandedly made it impossible for nature writing to lapse back into babbling brooks and heavenly birdsong'*

but in something far worse – its implacable indifference.' Indeed, Abbey dwelled fondly on the desert's danger, on how humans who neglected to bring sufficient water would likely find themselves pondering death, that their 'flesh will be working its way through the gizzard of a buzzard, your essence transfigured into the fierce greedy eyes and unimaginable consciousness of a turkey vulture,' a transformation that would constitute, for most, 'a promotion in grade.'[5]

Like many American nature lovers before him, Abbey asserted that modern, industrial people required regular exposure to wilderness, that living outside modernity's mechanized landscapes fostered independence and self reliance. But he had in mind a much more ambitious transformation than simply enlarging the amount of land set aside for recreation. The nation's much celebrated National Parks, after all, had become some of the leading victims and purveyors of 'Industrial Tourism,' places to drive through rather than to savour and to learn from. His solution? No cars or roads. 'We have agreed not to drive our automobiles into cathedrals, concert halls, art museums, legislative assemblies, private bedrooms and the other sanctums of our culture; we should treat our national parks with the same deference,' he explained.[6] The parks and the nation as a whole also needed more predators, fewer people. Sheep and dogs he would tolerate, but largely because coyotes liked to eat them.

Such pronouncements were not calculated to appeal to politicians hoping to be re-elected or environmental groups trying to convince mainstream Americans and law-makers of their reasonableness. But they resonated with youth grown disillusioned by the possibilities of political reform. Most of the radicals and reformers of the 1960s believed that they could redeem their society and its politics. The Vietnam War, a string of political assassinations, Richard Nixon, and the stubborn and growing conservatism of Middle America gave the lie to such aspirations. Not a few of the disillusioned 'turned toward the green tunnel of wilderness.' *Desert Solitaire's* pastiche of irreverence, macho individualism, and gritty transcendence spoke to them. 'A man wrote a book and lives were changed,' recalled one reader. 'That doesn't happen often.'[7]

Abbey's ideas were too undisciplined, contradictory, and playful to constitute a coherent set of environmental ethics. That task fell to Arne Naess, a Norwegian philosopher who coined the phrase 'Deep Ecology' in 1972. Naess contrasted Deep Ecology with shallow approaches, such as the pollution-oriented proposals of the 1960s which had focused on 'the health and affluence of people in the developed countries.' Deep ecologists instead urged a paradigm shift in which humans would recognize that they were part of their ecosystems. They preferred a '*relational, total field image*' in which organisms constituted 'knots in the biospherical net or field of intrinsic relations,' thereby dissolving 'the man-in-environment concept.'[8]

> *Deep ecologists instead urged a paradigm shift in which humans would recognize that they were part of their ecosystems*

Naess's prose was not always clear, and Deep Ecology did not immediately find a substantial audience. But his ideas spread in the 1980s, in part because he and his growing number of disciples laid out more clearly the philosophy's content and consequences. An eight-point platform began with Deep Ecology's foundational assertion: 'The well-being and flourishing of human and non-human life on Earth have value in themselves,' that were 'independent of the usefulness of the non-human world for human purposes.' It therefore followed that people should foster ecological diversity and had 'no right to reduce this richness and diversity except to satisfy vital needs.' This would require both shrinking the number of people in the world and their 'economic, technological, and ideological,' impact. This change could only occur if people committed themselves to achieving a higher quality of life 'rather than adhering to an increasingly higher standard of living.' We must realize that 'bigness and greatness' are not one and the same. Those who acknowledged the forgoing had a responsibility to walk the talk, to 'directly or indirectly . . . try to implement the necessary changes.'[9]

At the heart of Deep Ecology lay the realization that humans were not really separate from the rest of the world. This paradigm shift was necessary to turn western civilization away from the dead end of individualism and accumulation, the exploitation of other people and the earth towards a way of living that was at once more gentle and meaningful. 'When I realize that I don't have any independent existence,' explained Australian John Seed, 'that I am part of a food chain, for instance, then at a certain point Me-first and Earth-first become inseparable . . . "Myself" now includes the rainforest, it includes clean air and water.'[10] Unlike Leopold and Singer, who urged readers

At the heart of Deep Ecology lay the realization that humans were not really separate from the rest of the world

Arne Naess, 1912–

More than anyone, Norwegian Arne Naess is responsible for staking out the principles or philosophy known as 'deep ecology.'

Naess had a long and distinguished career before becoming the leader of an environmentalist movement. Born to a wealthy family, he began exploring Norway's landscapes at a young age. 'Because I had no father,' he later recalled, 'the mountain somehow became my father, as a friendly, immensely powerful being, perfect and extremely tranquil'.[11] Naess was also drawn to the world of ideas and in 1939 became chair of philosophy at the University of Oslo. He focused on science, semantics, and ethics, among other interests. But he also kept his mountain cabin and became a skilled climber.

Naess did not isolate himself from social concerns. He worked against the Nazis in World War II and for peace afterwards. Like many others, Rachel Carson's *Silent Spring* drew his attention in the 1960s, and he participated in a protest against a Norwegian dam and power plant. By 1968 his academic work focused on the philosophy of ecology.

Naess came to distrust the technical, human-centred solutions that dominated the early environmental movement. In 1972 he coined the term 'Deep Ecology' to express his belief that people needed to rethink fundamentally their relation to the rest of the world. Like most academic philosophers, Naess's writing and ideas are often hard to follow, and most proponents of Deep Ecology rely on more accessible writers. But Naess has frequently collaborated with these authors, and he believes strongly that environmental activism is part and parcel of Deep Ecology. He also counsels environmental activists – and everyone else – to repair regularly to wild places to find joy and engagement. 'Nature is overwhelmingly rich and good and does not impose anything upon us,' he remarks.[12]

to extend their ethics, their concerns to landscapes and animals, respectively, deep ecologists argued that we must expand our definition or understanding of 'self' to include the rest of the world.

For Naess, environmentalism is not primarily a moral imperative to repair the damage humans have inflicted upon the world. Deep Ecology invites modern humanity to consider a radically different way of thinking and living, to contemplate a way of being in which we join mountains and forests and other non-human entities in a life that will be at once more reciprocal and meaningful.

A philosophy so at odds with the central tenets of western civilization appealed to only a small fraction of readers. Indeed, moderate environmentalists liked to cite some of its more radical assertions to underscore their own reasonableness. But deep ecology elicited the allegiance of a growing number of environmental activists and thinkers across the western world during the 1980s and after, though many of them altered its tenets or emphases.

Bioregionalism became an important environmental movement in parts of the US, especially. Bioregionalists believed that ecological boundaries trumped political ones and that people needed to become intimately familiar with and committed to the landscape, the bioregion, in which they lived. They sought, in the words of an early platform, "to re-create a widely shared sense of regional identity founded upon a renewed critical awareness of and respect for the integrity of our natural ecological communities.'[13] A realization of humanity's place and stake in ecosystems would be fostered by concrete interactions with the plants, creatures, and other characteristics of specific places.

Bioregionalists formed – or, as they would put it, recognized – bioregions in the Ozarks, the San Francisco Bay Area, Cape Cod, and elsewhere. They touted the importance of consuming products from within one's bioregion and learning about its particular needs. Hence the Bioregion Quiz asked questions like where one's water came from and garbage went to, the annual precipitation, the material culture of the area's pre-contact indigenous

---

Gary Snyder, 1930–

Scholar, poet, philosopher, and environmentalist, Gary Snyder is often credited with anticipating the way of thinking that would be identified as Deep Ecology.

Raised in the Northwestern US, Snyder took an early interest in the outdoors and in the late 1940s attended Reed College, where he became part of a distinguished group of counter-cultural thinkers. He then took up Asian languages, worked at a variety of jobs, and studied Zen Buddhism in Japan. In 1969 he settled in rural northern California and soon established himself as a poet. *Turtle Island* won the Pulitzer Prize in 1975.

Turtle Island synthesizes the varied strands of Snyder's experiences and interests, from logging and hiking to ecology and Native American mythology to Buddhism. One poem is entitled 'Why Log Truck Drivers Rise Earlier than Students of Zen.' Snyder urges readers to perceive the natural world as linked to humans and their prosaic activities.[14] Tweaking Thoreau's well-worn phrase, Snyder asserts: 'Wildness is not just the "preservation" of the world, it is the world.'[15]

A leader in the bioregionalist movement, Snyder would have us recognize that we belong to nature and that our attempts to separate ourselves from it harm not just ecosystems but also our own lives and spirits. Unlike many environmentalists, who seek transcendence in nature, Snyder finds in this world a profound sense of rootedness.

peoples, its edible plants, and when the first wildflower bloomed. Like deep ecologists, bioregionalists combined a reverence for and knowledge of nature with a determination to treat it in a more sustainable manner.

Bioregionalists have insisted that nature is no place apart. The poet Gary Snyder, for example, in 1993 celebrated the work of 'watershed or ecosystem-based groups' that were finding ways to 'enhance wildlife survival' without turning areas settled by humans into wildlife reserves.[16]

Ecofeminism also located humans within rather than above or outside nature. They added a gendered analysis to this understanding, arguing that male values and institutions were primarily responsible for humanity's separation from and destruction of the environment.

Ecofeminists posited a biological and essential correspondence between nature and woman. Susan Griffin's *Woman and Nature: The Roaring Inside Her* and *Pornography and Silence: Culture's Revolt Against Nature* argued that men's abuse of women and nature was one and the same, a cruelty springing from a masculine fear of life and mania for domination. Rosemary Radford Ruether, another early exponent, asserted in 1975 that women 'must unite the demands of the women's movement with those of the ecological movement to envision a radical reshaping of the basic socioeconomic relations and the underlying values of this society.'[17] According to ecofeminists, then, women's body and culture associated women with nature both in fact and in men's imaginations.

> *Ecofeminists posited a biological and essential correspondence between nature and woman*

Ecofeminism

Ecofeminism emerged in the 1970s as part of the growing radical environmentalist movement. As its name implies, it combined feminism and environmentalism. Like so-called 'cultural feminists,' ecofeminists argued that women's biological and psychological processes made them uniquely close to nature. Western men's hatred of nature and women, then, resided in the same historical factors: western civilization's mania for mechanistic control and development, its denial of nature and the feminine. The solution to environmental problems lay in recapturing a feminine, non-domineering frame of mind.

Though more powerful inside than outside of academia, ecofeminism has provided a meeting ground for two powerful strands of modern protest and reform.

Like Deep Ecology, ecofeminism struck many as more philosophical than practical, but proponents tried to live out the philosophy. Karen Warren described how ecofeminism affected the way in which she rock climbed: 'One recognizes the rock as something very different, something perhaps totally indifferent to one's own presence, and finds in that difference joyous occasion for celebration.' The self and the rock are 'in relationship *if only* because the loving eye is perceiving it, responding to it, noticing it, attending to it.' Since 'the dismantling of patriarchal conceptual frameworks is a feminist issue, *how* one climbs a mountain and *how* one narrates – or tells the story – about the experience of climbing are also *feminist issues*.'[18] Gender also shaped how one tried to protect the environment. Some women members of Earth First! in California who found themselves on the margins of male-dominated protests decided to conduct nocturnal 'yarnings' in which they wound yarn – certainly a traditional feminine symbol – around and among trees they wished to save, as well as trucks and other logging tools. The loggers found the tangled yarn discommoding, or worse. 'This is the web of life, and when the web is cut, the spell is cast,' the women warned.[19]

If ecofeminists criticized Deep Ecology's neglect of gender, social environmentalists regretted its inattentiveness to class. Murray Bookchin, the movement's leading exponent, pointed out 'that nearly all our present ecological problems

> *If ecofeminists criticized Deep Ecology's neglect of gender, social environmentalists regretted its inattentiveness to class*

arise from deep-seated social problems,' and that therefore 'present ecological problems cannot be clearly understood, much less resolved, without resolutely dealing with problems within society.'[20] Like many other leftists, Bookchin found himself uncomfortable with the assertion that people were merely one among many species, let alone that they constituted, as some deep ecologists were wont to say, a 'human pox.' He argued that the modern exploitation of nature lay not in an androcentric culture, but in the dictates of modern capitalism.[21]

Many of these radical intellectuals were people of action as well as debate. In the 1970s they converged with veterans of the mainstream environmental movement who had become sceptical about the possibilities of changing the status quo through conventional politics.

David Brower led the way in the US. Raised in California, Brower began reading Muir at twelve and was an avid mountaineer by the 1930s. He joined the Sierra Club in 1933 and was soon among its chief decision makers. He played a critical role in blocking dams in Dinosaur National Monument and the Grand Canyon, leading the Sierra Club into an effective programme of public relations and lobbying at the national level.

But by 1969 Brower and the rest of the Sierra Club's leadership were at sword points. Many felt that he was going too far, too fast. Brower had come out against nuclear power, which most environmentalists then favoured. Years before he had proclaimed his allegiance for 'wilderness for itself alone,' and he had become very impatient with moderates who counselled patience and compromise.[22]

Upon being fired, Brower founded Friends of the Earth, which blazed a trail in radical environmental action. What distinguished Friends of the Earth was not so much the targets of its wrath, but its methods. Decentralized from its outset, local chapters were free to pursue their particular concerns. This grass-roots structure fostered creativity. The London chapter at first confronted issues ranging from mining to whaling. Then Graham Searle stood up at a public seminar and remarked: 'Well, I'm going to take my bottles Saturday morning over to Cadbury Schweppes,' the company that had just announced that it would not make returnable bottles. 'Anyone else who wants to do it can come along,' he added. The first effort was modest:

Graham Searle stood up at a public seminar and remarked: 'Well, I'm going to take my bottles Saturday morning over to Cadbury Schweppes,' the company that had just announced that it would not make returnable bottles about twelve handcarts of empty bottles. But lined up they 'made a terrific photograph.'[23]

Friends of the Earth was nothing if not media savvy. Cadbury Schweppes refused to budge on its policy, but widely published images of a sea of bottles brought waves of publicity, members, and money to the young group. When the organization turned its attention and efforts to the wearing of cheetah and leopard skins it spurned the back-channel deals brokered by groups such as the World Wildlife Fund and went public. Protestors bearing large photographs of slaughtered animals marched outside stores that sold furs. Sympathetic or simply intrigued journalists broadcast this message, and growing numbers of voters demanded passage of the Endangered Species Bill. Friends of the Earth excelled at bringing seemingly distant environmental issues home. One poster featured a garment made from the fur

Friends of the Earth

Founded by David Brower after leaving the Sierra Club in 1970, Friends of the Earth began in the US but spread quickly across the globe to become one of the world's most influential environmental organizations. By 1980 it had 250 chapters in Great Britain. By 2002 68 countries had chapters, with a total of some 5,000 local groups.

Friends of the Earth addressed a multiplicity of issues, many of them highly controversial: nuclear power, acid rain, trapping fur-bearing animals, toxic waste, over-packaging, and much more. Since it abjured non-profit status, it could lobby governments. This focus on influencing policy led to charges that the organization was becoming top heavy and cautious. But Friends of the Earth remains one of the most global and influential environmentalist groups.

of a large cat and this caption: 'Like the coat? The last owner was killed in it.'[24] British environmental organizations had been sensible and prim. Friends of the Earth was radical, confrontational, imaginative, even playful.

Success prompted Friends of the Earth to become more conservative. Its annual budget grew to $15 million, and in 1985 its US office moved to Washington DC to improve access to the federal government, a decision that prompted Brower to resign from its board, lamenting that his brainchild had become 'just another lobbying group.'[25]

> *Like Protestant sects, radical environmental groups tended to become more practical and moderate over time, only to be replaced in turn by new, extreme, organizations*

Like Protestant sects, radical environmental groups tended to become more practical and moderate over time, only to be replaced in turn by new, extreme, organizations.

In 1969 a group of British Columbian radicals tried to block nuclear weapons from being transported across the Canadian-US border. Two years later, after brainstorming over how to stop a nuclear test planned for the North Pacific, a member remarked: 'Why the hell doesn't somebody just sail a boat up there and park right next to the bomb? That's something everybody can understand.' The activists decided to do just that and, though deterred by the US Coast Guard and adverse weather, the spectacle of people willing to put their bodies on the line to protect the earth spread across the western world. Greenpeace quickly broadened its concerns to include whaling, seal hunting, and more – without losing its feel for political theatre and public relations. Film captured the drama of a harpoon from a Russian whaler passing within a few feet of activists who had positioned their boats between the whalers and their prey off the coast of California. 'For the first time in the history of whaling,' the *New York Times* noted, 'human beings had put their lives on the line for whales.' 'When you do an action,' explained an early member, 'it goes through the camera and into the minds of people'.[26]

Greenpeace paired vivid photography with direct mail to create unprecedented levels of environmental fund raising. Thousands and thousands of people opened letters to find photographs of baby harp seals being clubbed to death above the words: 'Kiss this baby goodbye.'[27]

Thoughtful Greenpeace leaders conceded, privately, that they were propagandists. Actress Brigitte Bardot's participation in the campaign against seal hunting transformed the story from 'blood and death' to 'blood and death and sex.' Nor did Greenpeace point out that whale stocks were recovering or that biologists found them 'about as sophisticated as cattle.'[28] Harpooned whales and bloodied seal pups tugged at heartstrings and brought results. The European Community banned the two main sources of seal skin in 1983, and whale hunting declined precipitously.

This combination of arresting acts and savvy marketing transformed Greenpeace into a behemoth. It spread from Canada to the US to Europe and beyond. Membership swelled to nearly two million by 1988, more than six million by 1994. Of course only a tiny fraction of these members engaged in direct action. But Greenpeace continued to conduct high-profile and imaginative actions. Banners protesting acid rain appeared on factory smokestacks across Europe in the mid-1980s. Behind the scenes and off camera, Greenpeace became an international player in negotiating environmental treaties and employed a growing number of scientists.

In the 1980s some of Greenpeace's most determined North American activists left the organization for a more radical one. Earth First! paired Greenpeace's flair for dramatic acts with scorn for anything resembling conventional politics

In the 1980s some of Greenpeace's most determined North American activists left the organization for a more radical one. Earth First! paired Greenpeace's flair for dramatic acts with scorn for anything resembling conventional politics. The organization's founders adopted the slogan 'no compromise in defence of Mother Earth.'[29] Believing that the planet teetered on the brink of collapse, Earth First! members argued that the time for tinkering with measures such as pollution control had long passed. They adopted Deep Ecology's embrace of all life, 'from virus to the great whales.' Asserted founder Dave Foreman: 'The only true test of morality is whether an action, individual, social or political, benefits the earth.' Like Edward Abbey, an inspiration and fellow traveller, Earth First! called for more wilderness, fewer people. Some went so far as to advocate forced sterilization: 'Education's too slow.'[30]

No politician in her or his right mind took these sorts of recommendations seriously, and some Earth First! members worried about the organization's misanthropic element. As the

1980s progressed, more and more members disavowed 'monkey wrenching' (sabotage) and advocated more strictly non-violent forms of protests, such as blocking logging roads. Many were put off by Foreman's apocalyptic vision of inevitable global collapse and argued that Earth First! could in fact play a role in making the world better – by forming alliances with timber workers to make logging more environmentally and socially responsible, for example. By the mid-1980s, Earth First! had become popular in spite of itself and had more than 10,000 members. Its growing profile drew the attention of the FBI, which infiltrated the group, and federal lawsuits. By 1990 Earth First! was in pieces – though many of those pieces remained potent. The group had remained decentralized and radical by design. In 1986 it had rebuffed people who had run Greenpeace's overwhelmingly successful direct-mail campaign. The organization remained 'a kamikaze operation,' as Foreman put it, intended to 'stir the stew,' 'to jolt the conservation movement out of its middle-age lethargy and re-inspire it with passion, joy, and humor.'[31]

In the early 1990s Earth First! members in England created a still more decentralized group, Earth Liberation Front, that began damaging mining equipment and bulldozers. In 1997 Earth Liberation Front allied with the Animal Liberation Front in the US and, a year later, did $12 million worth of damage at a Colorado ski resort. Other targets have included mink ranches, timber companies, and expensive homes.

Earth First! was not alone in finding itself divided over how to put its ideology into action. It was one thing to assert the unity of all living things, all entities on earth, quite another to translate that assertion into a political programme that would even begin to make a dent in western people's growing subjection of the earth.

Yet the radicals were not without victories. Thousands of university students and others have been exposed to the philosophy of deep ecology and its cousins over the past quarter century. The tactics of Friends of the Earth made the wearing of fur less acceptable and therefore less common in the West. Greenpeace won a global moratorium on whaling in 1982. Earth First! activists blocked the logging of some old-growth timber long enough for judges to issue injunctions protecting, at least temporarily, those forests. But these successes were, by the radicals' admission, modest.

> *Activists struggled to link the ethereal, even utopian, values of deep ecology with practical actions that would preserve the earth they professed such devotion for*

Activists struggled to link the ethereal, even utopian, values of deep ecology with practical actions that would preserve the earth they professed such devotion for. Like all radicals, they often found themselves pulled apart by the incompatible imperatives of ideological purity and political efficacy. Greenpeace, for example, enjoyed its greatest successes when it resorted to bloody depictions of animals that humans regarded as cute or noble – a tactic that alienated environmentalists who argued that anthropomorphism simply confounded humanity's regrettable tendency to care only for animals that reminded them of themselves.

Radical environmentalism was fracturing even as its adherents grew more numerous.

Recommended reading

A wide range of radical environmental ideas is presented and analysed in George Sessions, ed., *Deep Ecology for the Twenty-First Century* (Boston, MA: Shambhala, 1995).

Susan Zakin, *Coyotes and Town Dogs: Earth First! and the Environmental Movement* (New York, NY: Penguin, 1995) is a readable, incisive, and detailed treatment of radicals. Also useful are: Paul Wapner, *Environmental Activism and World Civic Politics* (Albany, NY: State University of New York Press, 1996); Fred Pearce, *Green Warriors: The People and Politics Behind the Environmental Revolution* (London: Bodley Head, 1991); Robert Lamb, *Promising the Earth* (London: Routledge, 1996); Michael Brown and John May, *The Greenpeace Story* (Scarborough, Ontario: Prentice-Hall Canada, 1989); Martha F. Lee, *Earth First! Environmental Apocalypse* (Syracuse, NY: Syracuse University Press, 1995).

Notes

1 Abbey, E. (1976) *The Monkey Wrench Gang*. New York, NY: Avon, p. 65.

2 Sale, K. (1993) *The Green Revolution: The American Environmental Movement, 1962–1992*. New York, NY: Hill and Wang, p. 29.

3 Singer, P. (2001) 'All Animals Are Equal,' in M.E. Zimmerman (ed.), *Environmental Philosophy: From Animal Rights to Radical Ecology*, 3rd edn Upper Saddle River, NY: Prentice Hall, pp. 31, 32.

4 Zakin, S. (1995) *Coyotes and Town Dogs: Earth First! And the Environmental Movement*. New York, NY: Penguin, p. 136.

5 Abbey, E. (1971) *Desert Solitaire: A Season in the Wilderness*. New York, NY: Ballantine, pp. 135, 216.

6   Abbey, E. (1971) *Desert Solitaire: A Season in the Wilderness*. New York, NY: Ballantine, p. 60.

7   Zakin, S. (1995) *Coyotes and Town Dogs: Earth First! And the Environmental Movement*. New York, NY: Penguin, pp. 38, 135.

8   Naess, A. (1995a) 'The Deep Ecological Movement: Some Philosophical Aspects,' in G. Sessions, (ed.), *Deep Ecology for the Twenty-First Century*. Boston, MA: Shambhala, p. 151.

9   Naess, A. (1995b) 'The Shallow and the Deep, Long-Range Ecology Movements: A Summary,' in G. Sessions (ed.), *Deep Ecology for the Twenty-First Century*. Boston, MA: Shambhala, p. 68.

10 Zimmerman, M.E. (1994) *Contesting Earth's Future: Radical Ecology and Postmodernity*. Berkeley, CA: University of California Press, p. 40.

11 Bodian, S. (1995) 'Simple in Means, Rich in Ends: An Interview with Arne Naess,' in G. Sessions, (ed.), *Deep Ecology for the Twenty-First Century*. Boston, MA: Shambhala, p. 26.

12 Bodian, S. (1995) 'Simple in Means, Rich in Ends: An Interview with Arne Naess,' in G. Sessions, (ed.), *Deep Ecology for the Twenty-First Century*. Boston, MA: Shambhala, p. 26.

13 Sale, K. (1993) *The Green Revolution: The American Environmental Movement, 1962–1992*. New York, NY: Hill and Wang, pp. 62–3.

14 Snyder, G. (1974) *Turtle Island. New York, NY: New Directions*, p. 63.

15 Turner, J. (1995) 'Gary Snyder and the Practice of the Wild,' in G. Sessions, (ed.), *Deep Ecology for the Twenty-First Century*. Boston, MA: Shambhala, p. 44.

16 Snyder, G. (1995) 'The Rediscovery of Turtle Island,' in G. Sessions, (ed.), *Deep Ecology for the Twenty-First Century*. Boston, MA: Shambhala, pp. 461–2.

17 Warren, K.J. (2001a) 'Ecofeminism,' in M.E. Zimmerman (ed.), *Environmental Philosophy: From Animal Rights to Radical Ecology*, 3rd edn Upper Saddle River, NY: Prentice Hall, p. 253.

18 Warren, K.J. (2001b) 'The Power and the Promise of Ecological Feminism,' in M.E. Zimmerman (ed.), *Environmental Philosophy:*

From Animal Rights to Radical Ecology, 3rd edn Upper Saddle River, NY: Prentice Hall, pp. 331, 332.

19 Gaard, G. (1998) *Ecological Politics: Ecofeminists and the Greens*. Philadelphia, PA: Temple University Press, p. 28.

20 Bookchin, M. (2001) 'What is Social Ecology,' in M.E. Zimmerman (ed.), *Environmental Philosophy: From Animal Rights to Radical Ecology*, 3rd edn Upper Saddle River, NY: Prentice Hall, p. 436.

21 Stoll, M. (2001) 'Green versus Green: Religions, Ethics, and the Bookchin-Foreman Dispute,' *Environmental History*, 6, p. 413.

22 Sessions, G. (1995) 'Ecocentrism and the Anthropocentric Detour,' in G. Sessions (ed.), *Deep Ecology for the Twenty-First Century*. Boston, MA: Shambhala, p. 170.

23 Lamb, R. (1996) *Promising the Earth*. London: Routledge, p. 38.

24 Lamb, R. (1996) *Promising the Earth*. London: Routledge, p. 63.

25 Sale, K. (1993) *The Green Revolution: The American Environmental Movement, 1962–1992*. New York, NY: Hill and Wang, p. 54.

26 Wapner, P. (1996) *Environmental Activism and World Civic Politics*. Albany, NY: State University of New York Press, pp. 45, 54; Brown, M. and J. May. (1989) *The Greenpeace Story*. Scarborough, ON: Prentice-Hall Canada, p. 39.

27 Zakin, S. (1996) *Coyotes and Town Dogs: Earth First! And the Environmental Movement*. New York, NY: Penguin, p. 308.

28 Pearce, F. (1991) *Green Warriors: The People and Politics Behind the Environmental Revolution*. London: Bodley Head, pp. 27, 30.

29 Sale, K. (1993) *The Green Revolution: The American Environmental Movement, 1962–1992*. New York, NY: Hill and Wang, p. 66.

30 Lee, M.F. (1995) *Earth First! Environmental Apocalypse*. Syracuse, NY: Syracuse University Press, pp. 39, 63.

31 Foreman, D. (1995) 'The New Conservation Movement,' in G. Sessions, (ed.), *Deep Ecology for the Twenty-First Century*. Boston, MA: Shambhala, pp. 54–5.

CHAPTER 7

Thwarted

LATE IN 2002 BEN AFFLECK bought a chinchilla coat for Jennifer Lopez. He soon received a letter from PETA (People for the Ethical Treatment of Animals) pointing out that the garment contained the hides of up to one hundred animals and detailing how they were electrocuted. A video describing the grisly process accompanied the letter.

Affleck, sensitive to the havoc PETA could wreak on his public image, assured the organization that the letter had 'opened my eyes to a particularly cruel and barbaric treatment of animals' and that he 'will not do anything in the future that supports it.' He also promised to write PETA a cheque.[1]

That powerful movie stars and models feel compelled to tread softly around selected environmental concerns suggests the growing power of environmentalism, a movement that became more professional and well funded.

But setbacks and division arose beneath the glossy advances. The largest environmental organizations – swelling budgets notwithstanding – compromised to achieve partial legislative victories. Conservative politicians gelded environmentalism even as they embraced it.

The number of people who identified themselves with environmental causes grew dramatically after the mid-1970s.

The shift was particularly dramatic in western Europe. By the mid-1970s residents of most nations rated 'protecting nature and fighting pollution' as 'very important' or 'important.'[2] Support for nuclear power declined dramatically after the Chernobyl accident in 1986, a disaster that scientists estimate will eventually kill several thousand Europeans. A 1986 poll found that 12 per cent of citizens in the European Community gave money to environmental groups, ranging from 4 per cent in Greece to 39 per cent in the Netherlands. One out of three Europeans considered themselves potential members of such organizations. Six out of one hundred had joined a local environmental action. More than two million people belonged to the National Trust, an eight-fold increase from 1971. The French, more wary of international organizations such as Greenpeace, had formed some 160 local or regional societies with about 850,000 members.

Western Europe passed the US in most measures of environmental performance in the twentieth century's last quarter. New technologies removed chemicals such as sulphur dioxide from industry. Britain's smoke emissions declined 80 per cent in the two decades after 1960. Biodegradable soap, recyclable packages, and other 'green

Western Europe passed the US in most measures of environmental performance in the twentieth century's last quarter

products' proliferated. People insulated their houses so that they would require less heat. Movements in Austria, Italy, and Germany halted nuclear-power plants. West Germany made the most impressive advances. From 1970 to 1995 it was the only major industrial nation to cut its per capita waste. By the mid-1980s the European Union's comprehensive environmental programmes were deeply integrated into its economic life.

Support for environmentalism cropped up in new places. By 1985 Italians were demanding solutions to industrial pollution, traffic, and other problematic aspects of the urban landscape. Bulgaria devoted 2.5 per cent of its 1986 budget to addressing pollution. Australia more than doubled its amount of protected land from 1978 to 1996. The number of Greenpeace members in New Zealand increased from 4,000 in 1985 to 170,000 in 1991.

International organizations had assumed a great deal of leadership in debating and settling environmental issues by the 1980s. Greenpeace, led by David McTaggart, transformed itself into a global player, as did Friends of the Earth. These groups tackled environmental problems in undeveloped nations, from logging Amazonian rain forests to poaching rare African mammals. They also addressed a growing list of global issues: whaling, oceanic pollution, the future of Antarctica, climate change, and acid rain. Much of the toxic waste emitted from US and German smokestacks ended up in Canada and Poland, respectively, and nations that imposed rigorous environmental controls on factories put their companies at a competitive disadvantage in the growing global economy with nations that did not.

The 1972 United Nations Conference on the Human Environment was a major marker in the globalization of environmentalism.

David McTaggart, 1932–2001

David McTaggart was born to a prosperous Vancouver family and later recalled days of 'absolute freedom' at a summer home on the British Columbia coast. The 'perpetually restless' youth pursued 'golf, booze and girls.' A string of jobs, marriages, and children followed, and by his early thirties McTaggart had become wealthy in the construction business. But success proved fleeting, and he retreated to sailing in the South Pacific. There, in 1972, he met some Greenpeace activists who enlisted him and his boat in the cause of halting France's nuclear testing, a practice that McTaggart resented for 'trying to limit my personal freedom.'[3] An altercation with the French Navy left McTaggart injured, famous, and with a new reason for being.

Blessed with passion, charisma, and considerable business experience, McTaggart soon took control of Greenpeace. He opened offices in Europe and cultivated contacts with other environmental groups and political players. His rare talent for combining radical positions with administrative expertise helped Greenpeace become both influential among policy makers and respected by uncompromising environmentalists. By 1979 McTaggart headed an international organization.

Characterized by a colleague as 'probably the single most exasperating, infuriating, obnoxious, obstinate man I ever met, and probably also the single most brilliant, charming, energetic, and charismatic,' McTaggart was no democrat. He brought order to an organization characterized by 'peace, love, and very little structure.'[4] His health failing, he resigned as Greenpeace's head in 1991 and retired to

Characterized by a colleague as 'probably the single most exasperating, infuriating, obnoxious, obstinate man I ever met, and probably also the single most brilliant, charming, energetic, and charismatic,' McTaggart was no democrat

his Italian garden, though he continued to work against whale hunting and nuclear testing, even as he feared that Greenpeace was becoming too large, cautious, and professional for its own good. Yet no one had done more than McTaggart to transform what had begun as a small group of radical Canadians determined to bear witness to environmental sins into a well-run organization of more than two million members which negotiated national and international agreements.

McTaggart died after losing consciousness at the wheel and driving into and killing the occupants of an oncoming automobile.

British economist Barbara Ward told delegates that they were taking part in 'one of those turning points in man's affairs when the human race begins to see itself and its concerns from a new angle of vision.' Representatives from 113 nations unanimously agreed that 'the protection and improvement of the human environment' was 'the urgent desire of the peoples of the whole world.'[5] Indeed, nations signed forty-seven international agreements regarding the environment from 1971 to 1980. The first major treaty came in 1987, when nations from across the world agreed on what proved to be an effective plan to reverse the earth's thinning ozone layer. Reports from scientists also called the public's attention to climate change, loss of arable land, declining biodiversity, acid rain, and the persistence of pollution across the globe.

So powerful was European environmentalism by the 1980s that it became the foundation of new political parties. West German leftists from peace, anti-nuclear, and other environmental causes coalesced in the late 1970s to establish the Green Party. They

Rio de Janeiro Earth Summit

The United Nations Conference on Environment and Development at Rio de Janeiro, Brazil, in June 1992 was the largest such gathering to date, with some 17,000 attendees, including representatives of 172 governments and many non-governmental organizations. It was also the most ambitious and it explored the interrelated problems of world poverty, development, pollution, and climate change. The government representatives agreed to join in a global partnership of sustainable development and pledged to reduce greenhouse gasses through ratifying the United Nations Framework Convention on Climate Change.

This agreement on how to stabilize climate change was refined five years later, at the United Nations conference at Kyoto, Japan. The great majority of western nations had ratified the protocol by 2004. But the world's leading producer of greenhouse gasses, the US (along with Russia and Australia), refused to sign, complaining that granting exemptions to developing nations such as China was unfair. Nearly all of the European nations who had agreed to reduce their emissions were, early in the twenty-first century, failing to meet their goals.

It remains much easier to espouse the principles established at the Rio Summit than to implement them.

established four key concepts or areas of agreement: 'ecology, social responsibility, grass-roots democracy and non-violence.'[6] The Greens spoke to marginal Germans. 'We will be a lobby for all those who have no lobby,' promised a

So powerful was European environmentalism by the 1980s that it became the foundation of new political parties

leader in 1983.[7] But their programme ultimately rested on their conception of people's proper relationship with nature. They desired 'a better, non-alienated life, in which the human being will be restored to his or her full creative powers;' humankind would 'give up its autonomy and integrate itself into the pre-determined cycle of nature.'[8] The Greens offered a radical alternative to modern, industrial society. They pointed the way to a way of living that was more humane and sustainable, just and peaceful – a sort of Deep Ecology for all.

It seemed, for a time, that the Greens might pull it off. The German party crossed the critical 5 per cent threshold in 1983, when they won nearly thirty seats in the Bündestag, West Germany's legislature. In 1984 they were represented in the legislative bodies of fifty-four districts or large towns. Late in the 1980s the British Greens won 15 per cent of the vote in a national election, the French Greens over 10 per cent.

But these successes were misleading. A vote for the Greens was not necessarily a vote for their idealistic agenda. The British and French Greens did so well in 1989 because they articulated a moderate programme. The German Greens were more radical but had the good (and short-lived) fortune to appear when West German voters desired an alternative to Helmut Kohl's ineffectual and corrupt government. But by the late 1980s mainstream German politicians were able to paint the Greens as extremists who would legalize drugs, free dangerous prisoners, and leave the country undefended by NATO or even a conventional police force. Unification, furthermore, brought into the political equation eastern Europeans who 'wanted more individualism, not less, more material benefits, not fewer.' Mainstream political parties learned to appropriate the Greens' most appealing ideas, leaving the Greens 'with the residue – radical, romantic and wrong.'[9]

Time also served to bring out often bitter differences among the Greens: liberals who argued for the use of market forces, realists who favoured coalitions with other left-of-centre parties, socialists who focused on the evils of capitalism, and hard-core ecologists who stressed issues such as conservation and animal rights. In France, too, the Greens split over whether to remain doctrinally pure or to pursue compromises.

Germany's Petra Kelly, the Greens' most prominent leader, was unable to turn her global celebrity into political power. The tedium of party debates tried her patience ('arguing and bickering among our various factions,' she

> *Germany's Petra Kelly, the Greens' most prominent leader, was unable to turn her global celebrity into political power*

called it), and her speeches in the Bündestag fell upon sceptical ears.[10] Many of her Green colleagues resented her fame, and they became angry when she violated party policy by refusing to rotate out of office in 1985.

The Green rubric served to bring together a diverse group of western European radicals, but that group remained both small and divided.

The popularity of environmental politics proved more fleeting still in central and eastern Europe. Bulgaria's first non-governmental organization dedicated to environmental protection appeared in 1988. Less than a decade later there were over 120. Opposition to the Soviet Union's assault on nature became part and parcel of growing unease with the Soviet leadership. The

Petra Kelly, 1947–92

Born in 1947 as Petrak Lehmann, Kelly moved to the US in 1959 after her mother got remarried, to a military officer from the US. She returned to Europe for graduate school in 1970 and by 1972 was an administrator for the European Community's Economic and Social Committee.

Kelly had a knack for getting the attention of powerful people long before she became famous. She corresponded with Vice President Hubert Humphrey, gained an audience with the Pope for her ailing half-sister, and, in her mid-twenties, had a passionate affair with Sicco Mansholt, the President of the European Community.

> ### Brilliant and idealistic, Kelly quickly became active in West Germany's feminist, anti-nuclear, and grass-roots environmental movements

Brilliant and idealistic, Kelly quickly became active in West Germany's feminist, anti-nuclear, and grass-roots environmental movements. In 1979 she left the Social Democratic Party to help found the *Die Grünun*, or Green Party. Kelly proved to be an electric speaker. 'She was sort of a controlled firebrand,' recalled an observer, 'disciplined but about to explode anytime – on a messianic mission to save the world from itself.'[11]

Kelly was good at bringing people together. She played a key role in creating and maintaining an international anti-nuclear movement and was optimistic that the Green Party could encompass a diverse range of political perspectives – though she was more reluctant than most green leaders to make deals with West Germany's major parties.

The success of *Die Grünun* in the 1983 elections thrust Kelly further into the public spotlight. She was elected to the Bündestag, participated in some high-profile demonstrations against missiles, and spoke to large audiences in the US. She championed many causes: children with terminal illnesses, feminism, Tibet, the rights of indigenous peoples in Australia and North America, women's rights, and, of course, peace. Her biographer explains that her reflexive compassion made her 'a magnet of non-violent principle trailing through the iron-filings of human misery.'[12] But more than empathy knit together Kelly's causes. She identified the 'power to dominate humans and nature' as the problem that had brought humanity 'to an impasse.' 'Ecology, social justice, nonviolence, feminism, antimilitarism, and anti-centralized structures' shared a motivation to dismantle hierarchy and domination.[13]

All the West German greens lost their seats in the 1990 election, but Kelly kept writing and advocating. In 1991 *The Sunday Times* named her one of the 1,000 makers of the twentieth century. A year later she died, evidently at the hands of a despondent Gert Bastian, her long-time companion and fellow green activist, who then killed himself.

1986 accident at Chernobyl sharpened criticism. Tens of thousands of citizens gathered to protest against nuclear power and industrial pollution. A demonstration at Kirishi, a city of 52,000 near Leningrad, began with a solitary father holding a black-bordered photograph of the dead infant child whom he claimed had been a victim of a biochemical plant's toxic emissions. He was eventually joined by more than 12,000 protestors. Residents of eastern Russia refused to let a

Residents of eastern Russia refused to let a nuclear-powered freighter dock in their ports. By 1990 over 300 environmental organizations had formed across the Soviet Union

nuclear-powered freighter dock in their ports. By 1990 over 300 environmental organizations had formed across the Soviet Union.

Politicians struggled to keep ahead of the movement. Soviet President Mikael Gorbachev won global acclaim by proclaiming at the United Nations that environmental problems affected 'the very foundations of the existence of civilization.'[14] Four out of five nominees for the Supreme Soviet addressed environmental issues in 1989.

But concern for the environment waned as the Soviet Union fragmented and Russia became more democratic. Environmental problems had underscored the old system's abuses and short-comings, but by the early 1990s attention turned to securing a livelihood: 'It is better to have a paying job and a dirty plant than to have neither,' explained two observers.[15]

East Germany's per capita sulphur dioxide emissions were fifteen times higher than West Germany's in 1988

Concern for the environment had dovetailed with nationalism in places such as Hungary and Poland, for Soviet leaders had buffered Russian citizens from the worst pollution by focusing much of the environmental exploitation in the hinterlands. East Germany's per capita sulphur dioxide emissions were fifteen times higher than West Germany's in 1988, for example.

Central and eastern Europeans became more aware of and vocal over these abuses in the 1970s and 1980s. Hungarians began objecting to the production and dumping of toxic wastes in 1977 and turned out in large numbers to protest against Soviet plans to dam the Danube River. Solidarity, the leading Polish independence group, embraced environmental concerns in the late 1980s. Polls found that environmental problems topped Slovakians' list of worries in 1990.

But, as in Russia, environmentalism fell with communism. Environmental organizations inside and outside of new governments found that economic growth routinely overrode their agendas. Researchers summed up the general public sentiment in the mid-1990s: 'a clean environment is a nice asset to have and maintain, once other more important needs are satisfied, namely economic.'[16] The conservative Klaus administration of Czechoslovakia claimed that environmental regulations interfered with the free market and prosperity. By the mid-1990s Greenpeace, one of the region's pioneering environmental organizations, had just 500 members in that country, and Czechs contributed just 2 per cent of the funding for its work there.

Concern for the environment had dovetailed with anti-Soviet dissent – it offered 'a training ground for democracy, a focus of anti-regime sentiment, and a foil for nationalism.'[17] But polluting factories were now controlled by East Germans, Hungarians, Poles, and Czechs, not Soviet leaders in far-away Russia.

Conservative, pro-business politics made a strong comeback across the western world in the late twentieth century. Great Britain's Margaret Thatcher embraced unfettered private enterprise and branded environmentalists as the 'enemy within.' Pro-growth, anti-regulation governments also took over in Australia and New Zealand in the 1980s. The Reagan administration infiltrated radical environmental groups in the US and dismantled much of the environmental legislation passed during the 1960s and 1970s. Promising to slash government and regulation to set private enterprise free, it cut the Environmental

Protection Agency by more than 25 per cent during Reagan's first two years in office. James Watt, who likened environmentalists to Nazis and Bolsheviks, served as the Secretary of the Interior. President Bill Clinton, a Democrat, talked in the 1990s of raising automobiles' fuel economy and taxes on energy use but quickly backed down from these unpopular measures. 'The USA featured by far the strongest connection between environmental values and core state imperatives around 1970, but that peak and American leadership are distant memories,' a group of researchers concluded in 2002.[18]

Radical environmentalists blamed their moderate counterparts for some of these reverses. The major environmental groups grew larger and more professional in the 1980s, even as their influence shrank. Representatives from some of America's largest polluters sat on some of their boards. The Ford Foundation provided funding to environmental groups with the stipulation that it could essentially vet lawsuits that the groups were considering.

Conservative politicians, like corporations, had learned to speak green by the late 1980s

Conservative politicians, like corporations, had learned to speak green by the late 1980s. Thatcher remarked that 'stable prosperity can be achieved throughout the world provided the environment is nurtured and safeguarded. Protecting the balance of nature is therefore one of the great challenges of the late twentieth century.'[19] Republican George H. W. Bush campaigned successfully for the Presidency in 1988 by pledging to echo Teddy Roosevelt's concern for the environment, and he claimed to have 'crafted a new common-sense approach to environmental issues, one that honors our love of the environment and our commitment to growth.'[20] This sort of rhetoric became standard among conservative political leaders who reassured mainstream voters that environmental protection and prosperity were fully compatible.

Conservatives had detected and exploited a critical difference dividing radical environmentalists from their fellow citizens. Most westerners evinced some apprehension over the environment's health. But they were prepared to sacrifice little, if any, material comfort. Germans have become the world's most passionate environmentalists. In 1997 they recycled nearly 90 per cent of the packaging material that they produced. But only the most determined Greens, a tiny proportion of Germany's population, have been willing to consume fewer resources than they could afford to. A small minority of Germans regularly use trains, and automobile use has continued to boom. Travel consumed about 17 per cent of German's energy use in 1950, nearly 28 per cent in 1997. Westerners seldom recognize that their environmental beliefs and behaviour are so profoundly at odds with each other. A poll of French business leaders from the early 1990s found that 94 per cent expressed a deep concern for the environment but that just 27 per cent favoured strengthening laws (by imposing

Sympathy for the environment ran high among the increasing numbers of people employed in the service industry, and such people tended to support the growing regulation of manufacturing, farming, and mining, activities that seemed to have little relevance to their own lives and livelihoods

higher taxes or tougher regulations) to protect that environment. Sympathy for the environment ran high among the increasing numbers of people employed in the service industry, and such people tended to support the growing regulation of manufacturing, farming, and mining, activities that seemed to have little relevance to their own lives and livelihoods. But these same people have been likely to both underestimate their own contribution to environmental problems and to resist government regulation of those contributions.

Wariness of environmental regulations has been particularly strong in the libertarian-leaning US. Advocates of more thoughtful and careful land use in the late 1960s and 1970s confronted charges that they intended to 'turn loose upon the hapless citizens of the various states a horde of planners and lawyers paid by the taxpayers, whose advancement requires success in preventing those citizens from making normal use of their own property.'[21] Cries of government interference were especially strident in the western US. Miners, ranchers, farmers, city administrators, and outdoor enthusiasts asserted their right to use or even take federal property. 'I intend to fight for my rights to use public land and wrest its control from their greedy paws,' averred a snowmobile and motorcycle rider.[22] The so-called 'Sagebrush Rebellion' morphed into a less confrontational Wise Use Movement in the 1980s in which a wide range of developers argued for fully opening up the nation's remaining natural resources. Neither of these campaigns represented the sensibilities of mainstream Americans, who favoured a significant degree of conservation and preservation. But distrust of government has resonated very well among US moderates.

Environmental progress stalled on many fronts in the 1990s. UK Prime Minister Tony Blair seldom addresses environmental issues. Public interest in and regulation of the topic waned in Canada. Mainstream American politicians commonly dismiss the problem of climate change altogether – or stress scientists' disagreements over it. Politicians who suggest raising its minuscule gasoline tax court disaster. In 2001 the average miles per gallon of America's new autos was at its highest level in twenty years. Despite pledges made at and after the 1992 United Nations' Rio de Janeiro Summit, greenhouse automobile emissions were up even among members of the European Union at the millennium's close. Growing numbers of politicians embraced sustainable development, a term coined at the 1987 World Commission on Environment and defined as 'development that meets the needs of the present without compromising the ability of future generations to meet their own needs.'[23] But this proved to be a highly malleable definition, in part because the World Commission was charged with drawing conclusions that a wide range of global and economic interests would find acceptable. The World Bank's 1992 report, *Development and the Environment*, denied that there were any 'fundamental ecological limits to growth.' Likewise, in 1995 the US Council on Sustainable Development called for 'changed patterns of consumption,' not less consumption.[24] Sustainable development, an eminently reasonable concept, has become another way in which harmful environmental policies are made palatable by framing them with green rhetoric.

Environmental doomsayers bear some responsibility for the growing numbers of consumers who believe that they can have

Environmental doomsayers bear some responsibility for the growing numbers of consumers who believe that they can have their environmental cake and eat it, too

their environmental cake and eat it, too. Alarmists of the 1960s and 1970s prophesied calamities that, by the century's close, seemed less and less likely to materialize – that the world would soon exhaust its supply of oil, for example. Environmental groups continue to exaggerate to gain people's attention – and money. Greenpeace recently asserted: 'It is expected that half the Earth's species are likely to disappear within the next seventy-five years,' a possibility that it privately acknowledged is remote. A Greenpeace leader explained, through a Norwegian reporter, their strategy: 'When most people do not feel that the world is about to fall off its hinges at any moment, they have problems taking the environmental organizations seriously'.[25] Indeed, Danish statistician Bjørn Lomborg's *The Skeptical Environmentalist: Measuring the Real State of the World* has generated so much criticism not simply because it may overstate the progress we have made in improving the environment but because scientists and others who measure environmental problems fear that acknowledging that progress will hurt their cause. But denying the improvements humans have made and exaggerating the problems that remain breeds cynicism and fatalism.

Conservatives across the western world have successfully depicted environmentalists as elitists. In hard-hit, timber-dependent communities of the northwestern US, bumper stickers appeared asking: 'Are You an Environmentalist or Do You Work for a Living?'.[26] Nature loving, as we have seen, has for centuries been associated with material comfort, and modern European environmentalists have generally belonged to what one scholar terms 'the new middle class' of young and well-educated people working in professions or the booming service sector.[27] A 1973 US survey found that 98 per cent of the members of environmental organizations were white and that 35 per cent were professionals. A majority of Sierra Club members surveyed in 1972 opposed engaging the 'conservation problems of such special groups as the urban poor and ethnic minorities.'[28]

It is not surprising, then, that mainstream US environmental groups at first overlooked or dismissed the toxic-waste movement. Cesar Chavez's United Farm Workers had begun pointing out the consequences of pesticides for Chicano labourers in California in the 1960s, about the same time that urban poor people began complaining of lead poisoning in their homes. Residents of Indian reservations protested against uranium contamination in the 1970s. The discovery of toxic wastes at the middle-class community of Love Canal in 1978 at last won the attention of major media as journalists swarmed to the site.

Thousands of local organizations devoted to keeping toxic wastes out of their communities formed during the 1980s. Hundreds of African Americans were arrested for trying to stop contaminated soil from being dumped in North Carolina. Mothers of East Los Angeles fought local waste-treatment plants. More than six hundred activists came together in 1991 to create the People of Color Environmental Leadership Summit and coined the term 'environmental racism' to point out that poor minorities bore the brunt of pollution.[29]

These groups differed profoundly from established, centrist environmental organizations. The CEO of a Texas company called them 'the most radicalized groups I've seen since Vietnam.'[30] Their leaders tended to be poor, people of colour, and women, often housewives, with little previous experience in politics. Juana Gutierrez, a grandmother of eight, led the Mothers of East Los Angeles. Unlike more mainstream environment groups, which largely fought rearguard actions in the 1980s and 1990s to keep existing legislation from being watered down or ignored, the grass-roots organizations broke new ground. Los Angeles groups stopped several projects, including a large incinerator. Such activists charge the well-funded 'Group of Ten environmental organizations' with continuing 'to support and promote policies which emphasize the cleanup and preservation of the environment on the backs of working people in general and people of color in particular.'[31] They are put off by the overwhelmingly white, middle-class composition of the boards of organizations such as the Audubon Society and the National Wildlife Federation and with these groups' poor track record of consulting with poor people who rely on extractive activities.

The new activists were not much inspired by traditional environmentalists' affection for wild places or radical notions of approaching the nonhuman world with a sense of kinship. They based their campaigns on human-centred problems that directly and immediately affected the health of their communities

The new activists were not much inspired by traditional environmentalists' affection for wild places or radical notions of approaching the nonhuman world with a sense of kinship. They based their campaigns on human-centred problems that directly and immediately affected the health of their communities. People such as Juana Gutierrez were fighting for their lives, for the physical well-being of their families and neighbours. This sort of self-interest led some to dismiss the anti-toxins movement as just another manifestation of Nimbyism (Not In My Backyard). But the strongly felt sense of danger that such activists shared galvanized people's energies in a way that most other environmental issues failed to do.

A similar trend began in Europe near the century's end. Earth First! and Reclaim the Streets! joined local residents to oppose road building in Great Britain, sometimes by direct action. Grass-roots French environmentalists also combined lobbying and civil disobedience to block proposed transportation projects.

The other sort of environmental organization to flourish at the century's end was organized on a much larger scale: the animal-rights movement. It, too, was international. In the mid-1990s Finnish activists attacked fur farms, trucks transporting animals to slaughterhouses, and laboratories that used animals in testing. People for the Ethical Treatment of Animals (PETA) appeared in the US in 1980 and spread across much of the world. Its motto was as simple as it was radical: 'Animals are not ours to eat, wear, experiment on or use for entertainment.' An observer describes its tactics as 'eighty per cent outrage, ten per cent each of celebrity and truth.'[32] Strategies include in-your-face advertisements, websites, and demonstrations. Parents outside a Barnum & Bailey Circus, for example, may find their children pondering large video screens showing elephants being tortured or even shot by their trainers.

People for the Ethical Treatment of Animals

Founded by Ingrid Newkirk, a British woman who moved to the US at the age of 18, PETA had become perhaps the most successful environmentalist organization in the world by the early twenty-first century.

PETA is more narrowly focused than groups such as Friends of the Earth. Newkirk's hobby is Formula One racing, hardly an environmentally friendly pastime. PETA focuses on human treatment of animals, and its approach to animals rights is both broad and relentless. Its publications and well-developed websites attack pet stores that take insufficient care of their animals; animal experimentation; circuses; factory farms; the fur industry; and fishing.

PETA blends idealism and pragmatism. Their leaders advocate and practise veganism, a form of vegetarianism that abjures the eating of any animal product. But they also work to improve the conditions under which farm animals are raised. They make extensive use of movie stars and other celebrities, in part because prominent people hesitate to ignore a group so skilled at capturing public attention.

McDonald's, the hamburger chain, and the voters of Florida recently decided to require people who raise chickens and hogs, respectively, to treat them less cruelly

PETA successfully exploits the growing gap between our first-hand experience and the actual extent of animal suffering. It gets donations of over $15 million dollars a year and has had some notable successes. McDonald's, the hamburger chain, and the voters of Florida recently decided to require people who raise chickens and hogs, respectively, to treat them less cruelly. More progress still has been made in Europe, where by 2012 chicken farmers will have to provide hens with perches and nesting boxes and sufficient room to move about.

The two most successful components of contemporary western environmentalism are very far apart from each other. The anti-toxins movement is based on human self interest, on people's health and very survival. The animal-rights movement seeks to jar people out of comfortable and familiar habits to take the lives of other mammals seriously.

Environmentalism arrived as a major political and social movement in the West during the 1960s and 1970s and proved its staying power in the 1980s and 1990s. A majority of people across the western world reported that they took environmental problems seriously. Membership in environmental organizations swelled. Government departments monitored and regulated pollution. Many large environmental organizations responded to an increasingly conservative climate by trimming their sails and lowering their sights, which created room for more radical organizations that sometimes enjoyed significant success. Environmental movements became much more varied and divided.

But environmentalism had not, at the millennium's close, much disturbed older western traditions: the desire for perpetual expansion, of ever-increasing prosperity and comfort. Most of us perceive no contradiction between environmentalism and growth. We therefore have a ' "light-green society": a polity in which virtually every activity is touched by environmentalist concerns, . . . without upsetting the existing state of things too much.'[33]

167

> *the most impressive environmentalist victories of the late twentieth and early twenty-first centuries occurred when activists successfully depicted pollution as an immediate, life-and-death issue for particular communities*

Indeed, the most impressive environmentalist victories of the late twentieth and early twenty-first centuries occurred when activists successfully depicted pollution as an immediate, life-and-death issue for particular communities. In the absence – or, to put it more accurately, perceived absence – of such threats, the overwhelming majority of western peoples at the millennium's turn were reluctant to undertake radical economic or social changes on behalf of the environment.

But the same cannot be said of environmentalism's cultural manifestations. By 2000 western people's enjoyment of nature had assumed increasingly extreme forms.

Recommended reading

Broad treatments include: Michael Bess's splendid *The Light-Green Society: Ecology and Technological Modernity in France, 1960–2000* (Chicago: University of Chicago Press, 2003); Russell J. Dalton, *The Green Rainbow: Environmental Groups in Western Europe* (New Haven, CT: Yale University Press, 1994); Kenneth Hanf and Alf-Inge Jansen, eds, *Governance and Environment in Western Europe: Politics, Policy, and Administration* (Harlow: Longman, 1998); Axel Goodbody, ed., *The Culture of German Environmentalism: Anxieties, Visions, Realities* (New York: Berghahn, 2002); Joseph Szarka, *The*

Shaping of Environmental Policy in France (New York: Berghahn Books, 2002); Douglas R. Weiner, *A Little Corner of Freedom: Russian Nature Protection from Stalin to Gorbachëv* (Berkeley, CA: University of California Press, 1999); Samuel P. Hays, *A History of Environmental Politics Since 1945* (Pittsburgh, PA: University of Pittsburgh Press, 2000); Joan DeBardeleben, ed., *To Breathe Free: Eastern Europe's Environmental Crisis* (Washington, D.C.: Woodrow Wilson Center Press and Baltimore: Johns Hopkins University Press, 1991); Jürg Klarer and Bedrich Moldan, eds, *The Environmental Challenge for Central European Economies in Transition* (Chichester: John Wiley & Sons, 1997); Mark Dowie, *Losing Ground: American Environmentalism at the Close of the Twentieth Century* (Cambridge, MA: MIT Press, 1995). Steven Bernstein, *The Compromise of Liberal Environmentalism* (New York, NY: Columbia University Press, 2002) provides a sceptical treatment of sustainable development.

Assessments of the world's current environmental status include: Bjørn Lomborg, *The Skeptical Environmentalist: Measuring the Real State of the World* (Cambridge: Cambridge University Press, 2001); Lyle Scruggs, *Sustaining Abundance: Environmental Performance in Industrial Democracies* (Cambridge: Cambridge University Press, 2003). The Greens are addressed in: Sabinevon Dirke, *'All Power to the Imagination!': The West German Counterculture from the Student Movement to the Greens* (Lincoln, NB: University of Nebraska Press, 1997) and Sara Parkin, *The Life and Death of Petra Kelly* (London: Pandora, 1994). The grass-roots movement is covered by Bron Raymond Taylor, ed., *Ecological Resistance Movements: The Global Emergence of Radical and Popular Environmentalism* (Albany, NY: State University of New York Press, 1995).

Notes

1 Specter, M. (2003) 'The Extremist.' *The New Yorker*, 14 April, p. 52.

2 Hofrichter, J. and K. Reif. (1990) 'Evolution of Environmental Attitudes in the European Community,' *Scandinavian Political Studies*, 13, 119–46, pp. 128–9.

3 McTaggart, D., with H. Slinger. (2002) *Shadow Warrior: The Autobiography of Greenpeace International Founder David McTaggart*. London: Orion, pp. 7, 8, 12, 49.

4 McTaggart, D., with H. Slinger. (2002) *Shadow Warrior: The Autobiography of Greenpeace International Founder David McTaggart*. London: Orion, pp. 93, 251.

5 Sale, K. (1993) *The Green Revolution: The American Environmental Movement, 1962–1992*. New York, NY: Hill and Wang, p. 41.

6 Bramwell, A. (1994) *The Fading of the Greens: The Decline of Environmental Politics in the West*. New Haven, CT: Yale University Press, p. 100.

7 Hülsberg, W. (1988) *The German Greens: A Social and Political Profile*, trans. G. Fagan. London: Verso, p. 100.

8 Dirke, S. (1997) *'All Power to the Imagination': The West German Counterculture From the Student Movement to the Greens*. Lincoln, NB: University of Nebraska Press, pp. 185, 192.

9 Bramwell, A. (1994) *The Fading of the Greens: The Decline of Environmental Politics in the West*. New Haven, CT: Yale University Press, pp. 110, 111.

10 Kelly, P.K. (1994) *Thinking Green! Essays on Environmentalism, Feminism, and Nonviolence*. Berkeley, CA: Parallax, p. 7.

11 Parkin, S. (1994) *The Life and Death of Petra Kelly*. London: Pandora, p. 113.

12 Parkin, S. (1994) *The Life and Death of Petra Kelly*. London: Pandora, p. 146.

13 Kelly, P.K. (1994) *Thinking Green! Essays on Environmentalism, Feminism, and Nonviolence*. Berkeley, CA: Parallax, pp. 37, 124.

14 Ziegler, C.E. (1991) 'Environmental Protection in Soviet-East European Relations,' in J. DeBardeleben (ed.), *To Breathe Free: Eastern Europe's Environmental Crisis*. Washington, DC: Woodrow Wilson Center Press and Baltimore, MD: Johns Hopkins University Press, p. 83.

15 Wolfson, Z. and V. Butenko. (1992) 'The Green Movement in the USSR and Eastern Europe,' trans. M. Toubin, in M. Finger (ed.), *The Green Movement Worldwide*. Greenwich, CT: JAI Press, p. 80.

16 Francis, et al. (1997) 'Conclusions,' in J. Klarer and B. Moldan (eds), *The Environmental Challenge for Central European Economies in Transition*. Chichester: John Wiley & Sons, p. 280.

17 Kabala, S.J. (1991) 'The Environmental Morass in Eastern Europe,' *Current History*, 90, p. 386.

18 Dryzek, J.S., et al. (2002) 'Environmental Transformation of the State: The USA, Norway, Germany, and the UK,' *Political Studies*, 50, 659–82, pp. 675, 679.

19 Jordan, G. and W.A. Maloney. (1997) *The Protest Business: Mobilizing Campaign Groups*. Manchester: Manchester University Press, p. 9.

20 Sale, K. (1993) *The Green Revolution: The American Environmental Movement, 1962–1992*. New York, NY: Hill and Wang, p. 77.

21 Rome, A. (2001) *The Bulldozer in the Countryside: Suburban Sprawl and the Rise of American Environmentalism*. Cambridge: Cambridge University Press, p. 244.

22 Cawley, R.M. (1993) *Federal Land, Western Anger: The Sagebrush Rebellion and Environmental Politics*. Lawrence, KS: University Press of Kansas, p. 64.

23 Bernstein, S. (2002) *The Compromise of Liberal Environmentalism*. New York, NY: Columbia University Press, p. 63.

24 Daly, H.E. (1996) *Beyond Growth: The Economics of Sustainable Development*. Boston, MA: Beacon Press, pp. 6, 14.

25 Lomborg, B. (2001) *The Skeptical Environmentalist: Measuring the Real State of the World*. Cambridge: Cambridge University Press, p. 18.

26 White, R. (1996) ' "Are You an Environmentalist or Do You Work for a Living?" ': Work and Nature,' in W. Cronon (ed.), *Uncommon Ground: Rethinking the Human Place in Nature*. New York: W.W. Norton, p. 171.

27 Dalton, R.J. (1994) *The Green Rainbow: Environmental Groups in Western Europe*. New Haven, CT: Yale University Press, p. 133.

28 Rubin, C.T. (1994) *The Green Crusade: Rethinking the Roots of Environmentalism*. New York, NY: Free Press, p. 230.

29 Edwards, B. (1995) 'With Liberty and Environmental Justice for All: The Emergence and Challenge of Grassroots Environmentalism in the US,' in B.R. Taylor (ed.), *Ecological Resistance Movements: The Global Emergence of Radical and Popular Environmentalism*. Albany, NY: State University of New York Press, p. 42.

30 Dowie, M. (1995) *Losing Ground: American Environmentalism at the Close of the Twentieth Century*. Cambridge, MA: MIT Press, p. 134.

31 Pellow, D.N. (2002) *Garbage Wars: The Struggle for Environmental Justice in Chicago*. Cambridge, MA: MIT Press, p. 75.

32 Specter, M. (2003) 'The Extremist.' *The New Yorker*, 14 April, p. 54.

33 Bess, M. (2000) 'Greening the Mainstream: Paradoxes of Antistatism and Anticonsumerism in the French Environmental Movement,' *Environmental History*, 5, p. 16.

CHAPTER 8

Extreme nature loving

'DO YOU WANT TO GO . . . where there are no crowds?' asks the advertisement showing a young couple preparing to cycle on a stark plateau overlooking deep canyons. But this is no brief for bicycling. The star of this advertisement is a Toyota 4Runner, the SUV (sports utility vehicle) that has brought the pair to this pristine place.

SUVs are the poster child of American indifference to gasoline consumption, climate change, safety, and the paving over of urban and rural landscapes. But these oversized vehicles sell like hotcakes, in large part because advertisers represent them as natural.

Most westerners had embraced both environmentalism and consumption by the twentieth century's close, and products or experiences deemed natural or wild constituted a growing part of their leisure time and disposable income, particularly in the US.

Wilderness, as we have seen, became a touchstone of mainstream North American culture in the 1960s as housewives,

Wilderness, as we have seen, became a touchstone of mainstream North American culture in the 1960s as housewives, accountants, even Republicans, grew their hair long, enjoyed John Denver's music, and otherwise cultivated a 'natural' image

accountants, even Republicans, grew their hair long, enjoyed John Denver's music, and otherwise cultivated a 'natural' image.

At the same time, technological changes made it possible for more and more North Americans to reach wild places. The spread of highways and other roads improved access. Nylon and other lightweight materials shouldered aside canvas tents and woollen blankets, and freeze-dried foods replaced bulky and heavy canned goods. Aluminium-framed backpacks enabled hikers to carry comfortably clothes, food, bedding, and shelter. Guidebooks proliferated, and by the 1970s a reasonably fit person with an automobile and a few hundred dollars for equipment and supplies could sally forth into the wilderness for a week or a day with little preparation or distress.

Millions of North Americans did just that. Traffic on back-country trails grew exponentially during the 1960s and 1970s until managers began to limit access to some areas. Hikers were no longer finding solitude. Those in New Hampshire's White Mountains ran across another person every seventy-three yards, on average, by the early 1970s. Good campsites were quickly taken, and disposing of human waste became problematic. A Forest Service employee at California's Mirror Lake reported: 'You literally can't find a square yard of ground without human faeces on it.'[1]

Radical environmentalists from Thoreau to Naess had asserted that regular explorations to wilderness were essential for modern humans. But well-intentioned visitors were, by the 1970s, loving these places to death.

Technology offered solutions. Minimal-impact camping emerged in the 1970s as a method to expand the carrying capacity of wilderness. Lightweight, portable stoves and foam pads made it unnecessary to cut wood for fires or bedding.

> *Lightweight, portable stoves and foam pads made it unnecessary to cut wood for fires or bedding*

Unlike their less numerous counterparts of the early twentieth century, who had taken to the woods to build shelters and trap animals, the modern, ecologically sensitive backpacker left no trace of his or her passing.

Minimal-impact camping

Minimal-impact camping emerged in the 1970s as part of the solution to overcrowding in North America's back country. It has grown in popularity as the number of backpackers in many areas has multiplied, bringing more litter, faeces, and erosion. Hiking and camping more thoughtfully could increase these areas' carrying capacities, allowing more people to enjoy them without degrading the environment.

Low-impact hiking requires staying on trails and wearing light boots. Low-impact camping entails using established camping areas and avoiding soaps or shampoos. Backpackers are discouraged from picking vegetation or starting fires. Excrement should be buried deeply underground, or, like garbage, packed out.

The goal is to enjoy wilderness without affecting it, to leave no trace.

But this emphasis on wilderness as a museum, a place to be visited but not touched, 'denied a working knowledge of nature.'[2] It also dovetailed perfectly with the burgeoning outdoor recreation industry. Camping without leaving a trace turned out to require a great deal of pricey equipment, a closer relationship with the very modern forces from which the wilderness promised a respite.

An even more expensive solution to finding wilderness emerged in the 1970s and 1980s: exotic ecotourism. Part of a larger trend in global tourism (which grew from about 70 million people in 1960 to some 500 million in 1995), ecotourism brought adventure seekers to remote and spectacular settings. The goal was two-fold: enjoy an authentic, wilderness experience without degrading its ecosystem. Both goals proved elusive. By 1991 nearly 40,000 western hikers were trekking annually through western Nepal, leaving deforestation, excrement, and erosion in their wake. A researcher in Belize, a small, Central American country, found that ecotourists seemed concerned with cosmetic problems, such as littering, and oblivious to the pollution generated by their heavy use of natural resources in travelling to and living in the tropical locale.

Unlike ecotourists, hunters made no bones about their desire to intervene violently in nature. The proportion of people in the US who killed – or tried to kill – wild animals had declined to about 12 per cent by the early 1990s, a casualty of increases in both urbanization and squeamishness over spilling other creatures' blood. The shrinking minority of hunters developed a new set of justifications. Some still used hunting as an excuse to gather with other men to 'drink beer, shoot at inoffensive animals, and talk about pussy,' as one indelicate observer put it.

Ecotourism

Ecotourism emerged in the 1970s and expressed the desires of many western peoples to enjoy exotic travel in an environmentally responsible manner, to consume nature and feel good about it.

In its pure, ideal form, ecotourism is environmentally and socially sustainable, meaning that it respects both the integrity of ecosystems and local businesses. It should promote environmental awareness and community development.

In its pure, ideal form, ecotourism is environmentally and socially sustainable, meaning that it respects both the integrity of ecosystems and local businesses

These goals have proved difficult to meet in practice. Simply getting to remote destinations requires a great deal of energy, and prosperous tourists generally create a great deal of waste. The ecotourism label, furthermore, is commonly claimed by businesses that are in fact disinterested in the long-term health of local ecosystems and communities.

But others articulated more esoteric hopes. They wished 'to get out into the hills, away from the crowds, to live, if only for a few days, beyond the wall' so that they would not become 'isolated from the natural world.' Killing was natural. 'I go hunting,' explained one, 'to have shadowy, sometimes violent encounters with my brother animals.' Taking a life forced one to confront 'the physical responsibility you take for the death of your food,' and 'the smell of the prey, and the feel of warm blood help restore our sense of belonging to nature.'[3]

Hunters and vegetarians perhaps share more in common with each other than with meat-eaters who pretend that chicken is a root crop. 'The [animal-rights] activist and the devout hunter worship at different chapels in the same church,' writes historian Matt Cartmill. 'Both long to break through the animal-human boundary, and both tend to see the wilderness as a realm of order and harmony from which the human species is alienated.'[4]

Other forms of outdoor recreation depict nature as a sanctuary. Rock climbing's popularity began to soar in the late 1970s. Like mountain biking and skiing, it offers thrilling, often dangerous challenges in wild, elemental settings. Climbing, explained one devotee, entails 'experiencing in a short, concentrated time the extremes of human emotion, the extraordinary joy in being fully alive, and the naked fear in facing up to great risk.' The uncivilized setting for these adventures is critical, for 'the personal encounter with wild and distinctive places enfolds the individual climbing experience within a deeply felt sense of the power of the landscape.'[5]

Backpackers, hunters, rock climbers, and other outdoor enthusiasts described intense, quasi-mystical, elemental encounters with a life force both beyond and connected to themselves, a confrontation that cut through the suffocating dreariness of ordinary, modern life. 'The world has become far too safe, and heretofore unknown lands are mapped in far too much detail,' explained one.[6]

Yet the wilderness's diverse devotees rely heavily on modern, often very expensive modes of transportation and equipment to stage their confrontations with primitive, unfiltered nature. North America's wild places have become integrated into its voracious consumer culture, have become a tour package of costly options from which well-heeled visitors extract experiences rather than minerals, meat, or timber. Fly fishing boomed in the 1970s, as new materials simplified what had been a very difficult skill. *A River Runs Through It,* Robert Redford's popular 1992 film, made thousands of

the wilderness's diverse devotees rely heavily on modern, often very expensive modes of transportation and equipment to stage their confrontations with primitive, unfiltered nature

converts, neophytes who flocked to stores where they 'bought high-end equipment, signed up for casting lessons, and booked their first trips to go fishing in Montana, Colorado, Utah, Wyoming, New Mexico, or Idaho – somewhere away from home, somewhere in the New West of the advertising brochures.'[7] Mountain biking followed much the same pattern. Bicycles with fat tyres and flat handlebars quickly multiplied in the 1980s, shouldering aside the old-fashioned road bikes with their narrow tyres and awkward frames. Most mountain bikes never encountered anything rougher than a suburban curb, but a significant minority of owners took to the woods to display their expensive equipment and physical accomplishments. Serious devotees moved to, or established vacation homes in, places with easy access to extensive trails, and mountain biking became a key economic component of many western towns and cities.

Fly fishing and mountain biking were purely recreational activities. The fishing was catch and release, not for food, and the biking was for fun, not transportation. Both activities required a substantial investment of money, time, and, often, travel. Like rock climbing or hunting, they occurred outside and away from the daily grind, the nine-to-five routine of life. David Brooks, in *Bobos in Paradise*, remarks that the search for authentic outdoor experiences draw 'the compassionate cardiologists from Chicago, the rugged realtors from Atlanta, the naturalist probate lawyers from San Jose. They've all found a place to recharge their batteries, smell the pines, and feel lonely and hard – in the summer months.'[8]

The American West as playground/retreat centre violates more traditional notions of how land should be used. In the 1990s environmentalists succeeded in bringing wolves back to parts of the western US over the objections of many local residents. Ranchers complained that wolves, like coyotes, would kill their cattle and sheep, that they were bad for business. Predators needed to be stamped out, pure and simple. More far-sighted conservatives warned that wolf reintroduction was a wedge opening the West to all manner of liberal and utopian interventions in western economies and landscapes, a step that 'will give environmentalists the tool they need to stop or appeal power lines, timber sales, road building, hunting seasons, oil and gas exploration, grazing.'[9]

> *wolves turned out to be very good for business. One federal report estimated that Yellowstone Park's contingent would bring about $43 million of business to the region annually*

But wolves turned out to be very good for business. One federal report estimated that Yellowstone Park's contingent would bring about $43 million of business to the region annually. Thousands of people, in fact, flocked to Yellowstone for the opportunity to catch a glimpse of, photograph, and, yes, howl with the creature that, in the words of historian Karen Jones, brought 'vibrancy to an emasculated landscape.'[10]

Most Americans sought wild animals under more controlled conditions. Southern California's Sea World, part of the Anheuser-Busch Corporation, assures visitors: 'Just by being here, you're showing that you care.'[11] But the nature that these visitors are invited to care about was in fact more than a little denatured. Sea World's famous killer whales are awesome, but affectionate, powerful but domesticated, part of Anheuser-Busch's corporate blending of the outdoors, leisure, and consumption.

The link between commercialism and nature is more patent at the West Edmonton Mall of western Canada, the world's largest indoor shopping centre when it opened in the early 1980s. Among the hundreds of stores resides a beach fringed by palm trees, a lake populated by dolphins, and hundreds of other animals, from penguins to peacocks, spider monkeys to piranhas. For a price, one can be photographed with many of these creatures.

A growing number of retailers were selling nature by the 1980s. The Nature Company by 1994 had 124 stores in the US and another 22 in Canada, Australia, and Japan. Their calling card was 'authenticity'. There were no talking bears on the Nature Company's shelves. One could find realistically rendered wild animals on T-shirts, calendars, note cards, key chains, and paperweights. CDs and videos featured authentic animals in natural settings. There were bird feeders and bat shelters, plus equipment to help one find and appreciate animals: field guides, walking sticks, and periscopes.

Historian Jennifer Price has brilliantly analysed the contradictions of the Nature Company and its imitators, places where we are urged to consume products made from oil, wood, and other natural resources in the name of saving the environment. We seldom think about the raw materials that go into, say, a CD of wildlife sounds because such products strike us as 'natural,' as unrelated to modern civilization and industry. 'The Nature Company,' explains Price, 'has billed itself as your direct connection to the natural world.' Yet this natural world has little of the feel of actual wild areas with their extremes of heat, cold, sand, and nettlesome bugs. Rather, one brings these talismans of nature, these sounds and photographs, into our most comfortable spaces, our climate-controlled automobiles and homes – where they serve as a critique of the very technological and commercial forces that made possible their creation and purchase. Purveyors of automobiles, perfume, tampons, household appliances, credit cards, beer, soda, and much, much more, made the same pitch by using wild nature to associate their products with 'Freedom, Adventure, Leisure, Tranquility, anti-Materialism, Simplicity, Place, the Past.'[12] If backpacking, fly fishing, or rock climbing had become consumer goods, then consumer goods had become nature.

Prosperous westerners more fully incorporated nature into their homes in the late twentieth century than ever before. The number of second homes in the countryside grew dramatically by the 1970s. About 7 per cent of Wales's rural dwellings, nearly 9,000, belonged to people who spent most of their time elsewhere. In Sweden about one out of every five urbanites owned a cottage in the country. Some million and a half people in France and three million in the US had a second home. Australians in

1984 noted that there were 'thousands of empty holiday homes along the coast,' in communities where many poor people were 'forced to sleep in cars, under bridges.'[13] The growth in well-to-do people's income in the 1980s and 1990s of course fuelled this trend. North America's

Prosperous westerners more fully incorporated nature into their homes in the late twentieth century than ever before. The number of second homes in the countryside grew dramatically by the 1970s

most beautiful resorts featured some of its most glaring social disparities, as low-wage workers serviced the needs of affluent, often temporary, residents. Many high-income people made their primary homes in small towns or rural areas, as computers enabled consultants, professionals, and business people to live away from urban centres.

Rural life offered access to nature, and nature offered liberty and goodness. 'I know all the woods, the fields, and it's part of me,' explained a resident of an English village in the late 1980s. 'Because I'm out in the country, I'm free.' Such residents, explains the sociologist who lived among them, viewed nature as standing 'apart from the selfishness, greed, power, and domination they see in social life.'[14]

Retailers have capitalized on this connection between nature and freedom by marketing replicas of rural life. Robert Redford became famous as a movie star who embodied the rugged individualism of the American West. Ensconced in rural Utah, he both encourages innovative films and peddles tokens of the Old West. The 2004 Sundance online catalogue features Redford's meditation on how the zen exercise of getting 'out of the traffic

Robert Redford, 1936–

Redford grew up in California, not far from Hollywood. He dropped out of college, travelled around for a bit, studied painting in Europe, got married, began acting late in the 1950s, and in the 1960s emerged as a star.

Redford strongly identified with Sundance of the outlaw duo of *Butch Cassidy and the Sundance Kid*, the movie that made him famous. The character, explains a biographer, 'fitted in with the actor's view of himself, on screen and off, as a sardonic renegade with emotional roots in the American west.'[15] He acted in or directed several other popular western films.

Redford's West is suffused by a sense of innocence. He insisted that *Jeremiah Johnson* be filmed in Utah rather than in a studio, as he wished his mountain man to express 'desire and sorrow for an unspoiled time and place.'[16] *A River Runs Through it* and *The Horse Whisperer*, both of which he produced, also celebrated an Old West of simple virtues and environmental purity.

Redford embraced the West off screen, too. He lamented that the 'green, open spaces' of his Los Angeles childhood had become 'concrete malls and freeways and the clean air turned into smog alerts.'[17] He made himself at home in Utah, where he could ride horses and ski. He made that place the centre of his creative enterprises by founding the Sundance Institute in 1981 and brought scores of directors and screenwriters there.

Redford believes that his West is threatened by the same forces that sullied Southern California. He has served on the board of the Environmental Defense Fund and the Natural Resources

> *Redford embraced the West off screen, too. He lamented that the 'green, open spaces' of his Los Angeles childhood had become 'concrete malls and freeways and the clean air turned into smog alerts'*

Defense Council and helped to block a six-lane road through Provo Canyon and a coal-powered electrical plant – which prompted the residents of Kanab, a town with twenty-seven per cent unemployment, to hang him in effigy. Redford's West is a place to be consumed through leisure, via movies, catalogues, and vacations, not resource extraction.

and into quieter calmer regions' drew him to 'the industry of animal husbandry. The life force exchange of moving milk from udder to sustenance was completely attractive to me.' Those unable to milk cows on a regular basis can presumably capture something of the same 'life force exchange' by purchasing a 'farmhouse stool' for $178.00 plus shipping.

But the countryside and nature are no world apart. Very human concerns such as nationalism, commerce, and social status continue to shape the ways we define and enjoy them. Nuclear power has attracted a great deal of opposition in the US but strong support in France because technological solutions suggest independence and autonomy to the people of that once-powerful nation. Residents of England have expressed a great deal of concern over the killing of whales; Scandinavians have regarded it as a traditional and therefore innocuous activity. By the same token, the British have resented continental Europe's concern over tainted beef in part because to attack its beef is to question the purity of its beloved countryside. Smaller landscapes are also shaped by highly anthropocentric concerns. Michael Pollan describes how garden catalogues lay out a richly textured mosaic of status and taste. 'From White Flower Farm or Wayside Gardens we can have a perennial border that fairly bristles with class distinctions, floral testimony to our soph-istication; from Harris or Park or Gurney's we can order a middle-class garden that proudly announces to the neighbors our family's enterprise, independence and togetherness; from Johnny's Selected Seeds or Pinetree Garden Seeds we can get a garden that reflects our environmental consciousness; and from Seeds Blum or J.L. Hudson one that proclaims our political convictions, in particular our zeal to protect the planet's genetic diversity from the depredations of big business.' A perusal of such catalogues reveals 'that, just beneath its placid surface, the garden is buzzing with social and political controversy.'[18] Nature loving more often reflects than challenges very human concep-tions of status and power.

Lawns remain highly popular, though maintaining the standard, mono-species variety requires large doses of water, fertilizers, herbicides, and pesticides – not to mention the pollution-spewing mowers that keep them looking tidy

Lawns remain highly pop-ular, though maintaining the standard, mono-species vari-ety requires large doses of water, fertilizers, herbicides, and pesticides – not to men-tion the pollution-spewing mowers that keep them look-ing tidy. By the early 1980s, people in the US lavished more fertilizer on their lawns than people in India used to grow their food. These flawless, homogeneous expanses of green continue to advertise their owners' capacity to create and main-tain a thoroughly unnatural sort of nature.

Much the same could be said of privately owned aquariums, stunning arrays of tropical fish, plants, and other living things that require a great deal of time, money, and, often, ecological devastation.

The Chinese had bred fancy varieties of goldfish for centuries when westerners started keeping fresh and saltwater creatures in glass containers in the mid-nineteenth century. The quality of aquariums and their heaters and filters and water improved steadily during the twentieth century, and by the 1920s freshwater aquariums were well established in western Europe and North America. Scuba diving and jet-powered aircraft made collecting tropical saltwater fish and invertebrates much easier after World War II, but keeping them alive for more than a few months remained problematic. The discovery of methods for establishing the nitrogen cycle (which transforms toxic ammonia and nitrite into relatively innocuous nitrates) and the use of live rock as a filter system made it possible by the 1990s for a reasonably well-informed hobbyist to maintain a diverse array of fish, corals, anemones, clams, and other oceanic creatures. The most ambitious set-ups included live sand and rock packed with small invertebrates (sponges, algae, and tiny shrimp and crabs) together with vibrant hard and soft corals, pastel anemones, brilliant clams and starfish, and, of course, a rainbow of fish. A full-blown reef-tank of 150 gallons literally brings to your home an approximation of the world's most dazzling ecosystem: the coral reef.

But a great deal of human expense, effort, and artifice lie beneath and behind these crystalline waters. To outfit that 150-gallon reef tank costs all but the most discriminating hobbyist several thousand dollars up front and a hundred dollars a month or more in electricity, replacement parts, food, and new livestock. Equipment includes not only a tank and a stand, but also lighting, heaters, a pump and powerheads to circulate water, a protein skimmer to extract toxins, filters to remove particulate and chemical contaminants, and equipment or kits for testing water quality. The dutiful aquarium keeper will change a significant fraction of the tank's water each week, replacing it with water that for several days has been mixed, heated, and otherwise prepared to precise specifications. She or he will also keep a quarantine tank in which to isolate specimens that have just been purchased (and may therefore carry parasites) or that show signs of disease. Keeping the occupants of a reef tank alive and attractive requires no small amount of expense, expertise, and vigilance.

It has become increasingly clear that the creation of countless miniature reefs across the western world and Japan has not been good for the reefs located in oceans

It has become increasingly clear that the creation of countless miniature reefs across the western world and Japan has not been good for the reefs located in oceans. Like zoo employees, aquarists can claim to foster an appreciation for nature. But the nearly 2 million marine aquaria in the world (half of them in the US) annually consume about 24 million fish and 12 million pieces of coral. Unlike freshwater aquariums, tank-bred fish constitute a tiny fraction (about 2 per cent) of the saltwater trade. The harvesting of millions of fish, corals, and invertebrates from the world's reefs has inflicted a substantial amount of damage. The dispersal of cyanide makes fish much easier to catch but causes mortality rates up to 90 per cent and can bleach or otherwise damage the reefs. Some rare organisms have become scarcer, and even commonplace species have dwindled. A study of the Yellow Tang off Hawai'i, where at least 100,000 are annually exported, concluded that this species and others were diminishing significantly and that the aquarium trade was playing a significant role. The removal of live rock near Fiji may be undermining the structure of its reefs. Live rock, corals, and fish are being cultivated in captivity, and some governments and organizations are attempting to regulate the ways in which marine organisms are captured. But these attempts are still in their infancy and do not appear to be keeping pace with the robust saltwater aquarium industry. A flourishing hobby devoted to the re-creation of breathtaking oceanic landscapes is playing a growing and apparently substantial role in the deterioration of such ecosystems.

Aquariums are small potatoes compared with the booming business of keeping dogs fed and otherwise happy. Readers of *Bark* and *Animal Wellness* magazines are confronted with a truly bewildering collection of goods and services. Dietary options include organic, free-range, and 'holistic dog food.' Dogs can sleep on beds (with choices of hardwoods) resembling miniature couches, and store their clothing, collars (which may include a 'Handcrafted Swiss' number), and other belongings in armoires. Health-conscious owners may be drawn to acupuncture, acupressure, insect repellent, sun screen, herbal concoctions to remove plaque from teeth, vitamins, antioxidants, and other supplements such as salmon oil that promise to decrease 'the risk of cancer development, severe skin conditions and premature aging symptoms like stiffness and lack of energy' (*Animal Wellness* magazine, volume 5, issue 5, 2003, 28). Travelling dogs may need seat belts, a ramp to get comfortably from automobile to ground, even goggles ('doggles') to protect the eyes of dogs who like to stick their heads out of car windows. Services include pet photographers and painters and dog-oriented summer camps, bed and breakfasts, and motels. Other products and services speak to dogs' emotional or psychological well-being: anti-depressants, yoga, reiki, aromatherapy, Anxiety Wraps to calm pets during thunderstorms, and herb-laced chew bones 'designed to gently calm dogs without sedating them.' Sue Becker, a specialist in 'Interspecies Communication', offers to help pets overcome 'problems and stress, improve behaviour, deepen understanding and your relationship.' Such services do not end at death. Bereaved owners can purchase Furry Angel Pet Memorial candles, urns for ashes, and memorial stones in the likeness of one's departed friend. Sharon Callahan, author of *Healing Animals Naturally with Flower Essences*, recalls how a terminally ill cat, Tangie, allowed Callahan to be her voice 'so she could help her family better understand what was happening to her and what action they should take on her behalf.' Tangie made it known that she wanted to 'lie in her favorite spot surrounded by candles and sacred pictures,' to be sung to, hear some stories, and to be buried in nature.[19]

Pet magazines proclaim that cats and especially dogs are as important as people. Indeed, increasing numbers of owners are paying thousands of dollars on surgical procedures once reserved for humans

Pet magazines proclaim that cats and especially dogs are as important as people. Indeed, increasing numbers of owners are paying thousands of dollars on surgical procedures once reserved for humans. Americans spent about $19 billion on pet care in 2002, nearly twice what they spent in the mid-1990s.

Jon Katz, who writes for *The New York Times* and *Bark*, among other publications, argues in *The New Work of Dogs: Tending to Life, Love, and Family* that more and more Americans find their primary companionship with canines. Dogs have assumed therapeutic roles with people who are near death or severely disturbed. But most of their new work occurs with more ordinary folk, particularly the growing proportion of the population who live alone. About one third of people in an American Animal Hospital Association survey report that they rely more heavily on their pets for affection and companionship than on people. Katz describes a woman disappointed by men and work who at last found, in a dachshund, 'raw, pure, completely unconditional love;' a driven attorney emotionally estranged from his children and wife who proclaimed that his Labrador would 'take a bullet for me;' a sensitive youth who looked to his pit bull for both friendship and credibility in his tough neighbourhood; a group of women who turned to dogs to nurture them through divorce; lonely seniors whose only reliable companions were their pets. 'She's all I have now,' said a widower of his little dog. 'Everyone else is gone.'[20]

The New Work of Dogs is often a depressing book, though the reader is apt to feel a certain gratitude for the plucky pets gamely bolstering a sagging social structure once maintained by spouses, children, other kin, friends, neighbours, churches, fraternal orders, and bowling leagues.

But these pets are often injured by our social expectations. Dogs may be steadfast, but people are not. The woman who loved her dachshund so much that she could not bear to potty train it eventually grew weary of and irritated with her ill-mannered pet. The boy who had relied on his pit bull for status sent it to the pound after he made the basketball team. Katz found that even much-beloved dogs often suffered from their owners' ignorance, especially regarding the amount of exercise that they required. This sort of negligence, and the frustration that it fosters, helps explain why close to 10 million dogs a year are sent to shelters, where about half of them will be killed.

Americans have continued to view wild animals as pets. *Free Willy* describes a troubled boy's friendship with a killer whale. Life soon imitated art, as thousands of children and not a few adults became determined to free Keiko, who had played 'Willy,' from captivity in a Mexico theme park.

> *Millions of dollars were spent to return Keiko to the North Atlantic – where he soon died*

Millions of dollars were spent to return Keiko to the North Atlantic – where he soon died. Critics pointed out that the time and money spent on Keiko could have gone to more substantial conservation efforts. Nor were Keiko's most devoted fans of one mind about freeing him. In the movie that made him famous, Willy's most intense relationship is, after all, with a boy, and when he swims away at the end, we are not sure whether to cheer or to weep. Hence the film generated both protests of and visits to Sea World, which holds in captivity the largest collection of killer whales. We want animals to be simultaneously free and friendly.

Finding Nemo, a 2003 film, generates the same paradoxical reactions. Nemo is a young clownfish who strays from his overprotective father and is then netted by a diver who confines him

Keiko, late 1970s–2003

Born near Iceland, this killer whale was captured in 1979. By 1985 it was in a small amusement park in Mexico City.

A few years later Keiko's life was transformed when the makers of *Free Willy* selected it to star in a film about a troubled boy who became a killer whale's friend and liberator. The movie did well, particularly with children, and thousands of viewers began taking an interest in saving whales – particularly 'Willy.' Early in 1996 Mexican children cried as Keiko flew north to the Oregon Coast Aquarium, where the Free Willy/Keiko Foundation had constructed a $7.3 million tank for him.

Keiko proved to be an economic boon for the struggling aquarium and the tourist-oriented businesses around it, and in 1997 the aquarium went to court to keep their meal ticket from being returned to the ocean, as the foundation had promised. But Keiko at last went home to Iceland a year later, where he spent most of his time in an enclosed bay where he was closely monitored. In 2002 he at last decided to join a pod of killer whales, though he caused his devotees no small amount of alarm by perversely making his way to Norway, the only European country to allow whaling. Keiko's keepers moved their operations from Iceland and again tended to and fed the creature that seemed determined to spend his time with humans rather than killer whales. It soon died, evidently of pneumonia, and was buried on a beach in Norway.

Keiko stirred controversy even in death. Early in 2004 the Norwegian Organization for the Conservation of Nature claimed that its rotting six-ton carcass would release dangerous amounts of cancer-causing toxins into the local ecosystem. The environmental group admitted that the toxins probably did not represent a serious threat but hoped that the publicity generated by their announcement would draw people's attention to oceanic pollution.

Some children flushed their pets down the toilet in the misplaced hope that they, like Nemo, would rejoin their families in the freedom of the ocean

to his dental-office tank. Nemo's father then ventures from his home to retrieve his son, who escapes from the tank by feigning death and getting flushed down the toilet. The popular movie prompted both criticism of salt-water fish keeping and a boom in that business. Some children flushed their pets down the toilet in the misplaced hope that they, like Nemo, would rejoin their families in the freedom of the ocean.

Our concern for animals on film or television has become so great that dozens of viewers called to protest against the killing of a mouse in *The Green Mile*. They were relieved to learn that the mouse was computer generated. Indeed, the industry spends a great deal of time and money meeting the standards of the American Humane's Film and Television Unit. One can do only three takes a day of a fish, for example, and no animals, including cockroaches or worms, are to be harmed – though actors and actresses are, of course, free to squish insects off the set.

Our views and uses of animals are a wonderful metaphor for and microcosm of modern nature loving. Pets, like mountains or sea anemones, do not talk back. If our dog licks our wounds, it will not assert that it does so not out of love but because it likes the taste of blood. If we spend our precious money and time to trek to the Himalayas, those mountains will not remark that they would just as soon we stayed home and took a walk in our neighbourhood.

Because dogs and mountains do not speak, nature loving can mean whatever we wish it to. We can express our allegiance to it by backpacking, hunting, rock climbing, fly fishing, howling with the wolves, buying a poster of a howling wolf, gardening, buying a second house in the country, going to the West Edmonton Mall, or keeping a reef tank or a German Shepherd. In our postmodern, atomistic western world, environmentalism, like truth and beauty, is in the eye of the beholder.

In all of these activities, moreover, we consume nature – sometimes acutely – even as we celebrate it. Modern nature loving often entails harming the environment as we establish our sensitivity to it.

Recommended reading

Various aspects of modern nature loving are treated by: David Nicholson-Lord, *The Greening of the Cities* (London: Routledge & Kegan Paul, 1987); Susan G. Davis, *Spectacular Nature: Corporate Culture and the Sea World Experience* (Berkeley, CA: University of California Press, 1997); Colette Wabnitz, et al, *The Global Trade in Marine Ornamental Species* (Cambridge: UNEP World Conservation Monitoring Centre, 2003). Jon Katz's *The New Work of Dogs: Tending to Life, Love, and Family* (New York: Villard, 2003) is extremely useful, as is Liza Nicholas, Elaine M. Bapis, and Thomas J. Harvey, eds, *Imagining the Big Open: Nature, Identity, and Play in the New West* (Salt Lake City, UT: University of Utah Press, 2003), which treats some aspects of extreme sports, as does Robert E. Rinehart and Synthia Sydnor, eds, *To the Extreme: Alternative Sports, Inside and Out* (Albany, NY: State University of New York Press, 2003. Rosaleen Duffy, *A Trip Too Far: Ecotourism, Politics, and Exploitation* (London: Earthscan, 2002) and Erlet Cater and Gwen Lowman, *Ecotourism: A Sustainable Option*

(Chichester: John Wiley & Sons, 1994) analyse ecotourism. Jennifer Price's *Flight Maps: Adventures with Nature in Modern America* (New York, NY: Basic) is splendid cultural history.

Notes

1   Nash, R.F. (2001) *Wildeness and the American Mind*. 4th edn New haven, CT: Yale University Press, p. 320.

2   Turner, J.M. (2002) 'From Woodcraft to "Leave No Trace": Wilderness, Consumerism, and Environmentalism in Twentieth-Century America,' Environmental History, 7, p. 476.

3   Cartmill, M. (1993) *A View to Death in the Morning: Hunting and Nature through History*. Cambridge, MA: Harvard University Press, pp. 233–6.

4   Cartmill, M. (1993) *A View to Death in the Morning: Hunting and Nature through History*. Cambridge, MA: Harvard University Press, pp. 235–6.

5   Rex-Atzet, W. (2003) 'Narratives of Place and Power: Laying Claim to Devils Tower,' in L. Nicholas, et al (eds), *Imagining the Big Open: Nature, Identity, and Play in the New West*. Salt Lake City, UT: University of Utah Press, p. 54.

6   Watters, R. (2003) 'The Wrong Side of the Thin Edge,' in R.E. Rinehart and S. Sydnor (eds), *To the Extreme: Alternative Sports, Inside and Out*. Albany, NY: State University of New York Press, p. 259.

7   Owens, K. (2003) 'Fishing the Hatch: New West Romanticism and Fly-Fishing in the High Country,' in L. Nicholas, et al (eds), *Imagining the Big Open: Nature, Identity, and Play in the New West*. Salt Lake City, UT: University of Utah Press, p. 118.

8   Brooks, D. (2000) *Bobos in Paradise: The New Upper Class and How They Got There*. New York, NY: Simon & Schuster, p. 220.

9   Jones, K. (2003) 'Way Out West . . . Ghost Towns, Gray Wolves, Territorial Prisons & More! Celebrating the Wolf in the New West,'

in L. Nicholas, et al (eds), *Imagining the Big Open: Nature, Identity, and Play in the New West*. Salt Lake City, UT: University of Utah Press, p. 39.

10 Jones, K. (2003) 'Way Out West . . . Ghost Towns, Gray Wolves, Territorial Prisons & More! Celebrating the Wolf in the New West,' in L. Nicholas, et al (eds), *Imagining the Big Open: Nature, Identity, and Play in the New West*. Salt Lake City, UT: University of Utah Press, p. 36.

11 Davis, S.G. (1997) *Spectacular Nature: Corporate Culture and the Sea World Experience*. Berkeley, CA: University of California Press, p. 228.

12 Price, J. (1999) *Flight Maps: Adventures with Nature in Modern America*. New York, NY: Basic Books, pp. 174, 237.

13 Brown, N. (1998) 'On the Margins of the Littoral Society: The New South Wales South Coast since 1945,' 2, p. 214.

14 Bell, M.M. (1994) *Childerley: Nature and Morality in a Country Village*. Chicago, IL: University of Illinois Press, pp. 137, 138.

15 Clinch, M. (1989) *Robert Redford*. London: Hodder & Stoughton, p. 72.

16 Bapis, E.M. (2003) 'Scripting the West: Robert Redford's Persona and Films,' in L. Nicholas, et al (eds), *Imagining the Big Open: Nature, Identity, and Play in the New West*. Salt Lake City, UT: University of Utah Press, p. 247.

17 Redford, R. (1991) 'Introduction,' in Porrit, (ed.), *Save the Earth*. Atlanta, GA: Turner Publishing, p. 10.

18 Pollan, M. (1991) *Second Nature: A Gardener's Education*. New York, NY: Dell, pp. 242–3.

19 Callahan, S. (2003) 'Communing with Animals: Tangie's Transition,' *Animal Wellness Magazine*, 5, 4, p. 50.

20 Katz, J. (2003) *The New Work of Dogs: Tending to Life, Love, and Family*. New York, NY: Villard, pp. 37, 85, 172.

Conclusion

'We live in an old chaos of the sun . . .'
Wallace Stevens, 'Sunday Morning'

NATURE LOVING HAS SERVED a dizzying number of ends over the past several centuries: nostalgia; status; nationalism; sociability; various strains of radicalism; or simply the desire to construct or inhabit, for an hour or a lifetime, a perfect place.

Prosperity has been the common denominator of our varied expressions of affection and concern for the non-human environment. Our worries over nature have risen with capitalism and a steadily increased material standard of living. They quickened during the Renaissance, intensified during the Enlightenment of the eighteenth century, reached the growing middle class of the industrializing nineteenth and early twentieth centuries, then became a major cultural and political force with the arrival of unprecedented levels of affluence in the 1960s. Environmentalism worked its way into culture through poetry, prose, gardens, pet keeping, music, and religion. But it also spawned powerful political movements that regulated the extraction of natural resources; protected selected vistas, fauna and flora, and ecosystems; and dramatically reduced some types of pollution.

The association between prosperity and nature loving can be traced between nations as well as over time. England was much more concerned with preserving its countryside and cherished animals

The association between prosperity and nature loving can be traced between nations as well as over time

than continental Europe at the peak of England's political and economic power, from the nineteenth century until World War II. Western nature preservation and pollution controls alike have lagged behind after World War II in the places with the most rudimentary economies: the Soviet Union and its satellites, of course, but also Spain, Italy, Greece, and Ireland. The same generalization can be made within nations. Environmental activists, like other reformers, have tended to be young, but they have also been well-educated, often prosperous. Well-to-do nations and people have been most likely to express an affinity and concern for nature. Environmentalism has been the child of affluence.

There is a positive correlation between prosperity and environmental achievement in areas such as pollution control, water treatment, and recycling. Hence West Germany, Sweden, the Netherlands, and Denmark rate much higher in these areas than do Ireland, Spain, and Italy.

But at some point rising per capita income 'is associated with declining performance.'[1] Canada and especially the US are the leading examples of this phenomenon. Indeed, a 2003 study of twenty-one powerful countries placed the US last in global environmental stewardship, with Canada and Australia also ranking in the bottom four. In 1990 the average US urban resident drove 16,045 kilometres and used public transport for just 474. In Europe the figures were much closer: 6,601 kilometres by auto and 1,895 by public transport. Canada and Australia fell between the US and Europe.

Prosperous nations have been reluctant to protect the environment at the risk of undermining the pursuit of prosperity that has resided at the centre of the modern western world for the past several centuries. Environmental improvements that can be had through technological innovations, such as catalytic converters, are one thing. Driving less is quite another. Hence pollutants such as sulphur dioxide have fallen even as the amount of gasoline burned has soared, but carbon dioxide, which has proved much more difficult to extract from internal-combustion engines, has continued to rise. Rich nations and their citizens have been unwilling to curtail their consumption of resources.

> *Rich nations and their citizens have been unwilling to curtail their consumption of resources*

This commitment to prosperity has existed alongside a professed and growing commitment to nature. By the 1990s, more than four out of five people in the US identified themselves as environmentalists. In France, writes historian Michael Bess, 'practically every nook and cranny of French society eventually came to acquire an environmentalist tint.' But this sentiment 'ran shallow and wide' and constituted a sort of 'light-green society' in which people have wanted both 'all the comforts of material abundance and the cheery prospect of limitless economic expansion' and 'a safe, clean, verdant environment in which to enjoy these boons.'[2]

Freedom and individualism reconcile this contradiction, this simultaneous embrace of nature and prosperity. We are willing to preserve places and animals associated with freedom: mountains, ocean shores, eagles, wolves, whales, and other 'charismatic megafauna.' But our commitment to individual rights undercuts attempts to slow, let alone reverse, the growing pressure humanity is putting on the rest of the world through population growth, larger homes, increased automobile use, and general consumption. Automobiles, like nature, make us feel free, which is why automobile advertisements so frequently place their products in wild places. One would be hard put to identify a more environmentally damaging activity than driving. Automobiles gobble oil, metals, and other resources, create a great deal of pollution, require the paving of land, and kill untold numbers of people and other animals. But we associate automobiles, like mountains and birds, with boundlessness.

That so few of us consistently perceive a contradiction between our allegiance to material comfort and environmental health owes something to human nature and frailties, to our ample capacity for ignoring inconvenient truths.

That so few of us consistently perceive a contradiction between our allegiance to material comfort and environmental health owes something to human nature and frailties, to our ample capacity for ignoring inconvenient truths

201

Many of us are also confused by the apparent lack of scientific consensus on whether and exactly how the environment is declining and precisely what must or ought to be done to improve matters. In the US, for example, no small number of highly educated and influential people profess to believe that global warming is a myth and that government measures to improve fuel efficiency would constitute an unwarranted attack on the liberty of the individual. President George W. Bush has a particularly remarkable record of ignoring or denying acute environmental problems. That not a few environmentalists have issued prophesies that have been at once apocalyptic and absurd has served to discredit reasonable and credible warnings.

But our capacity to increase our consumption of nature even as we express affection and concern for it also depends on our ability to compartmentalize these two elements of our lives, our practice and our beliefs. Susan Davis's fine analysis of Sea World points out that the San Diego theme park depicts nature as 'remote, pure, balanced, and teeming with life' while reassuring us 'that nature is going to be all right.'[3] Indeed, many of our self-conscious encounters with nature serve to affirm our ecological sensitivity while disguising the ways in which these very encounters contribute to ecological problems. One thinks of the ecotourists who pump massive amounts of waste into air, land, and sea to arrive and live at exotic and remote locales where they avoid violating the repose of a blade of grass or piece of coral. Modern westerners have become extremely isolated from the natural processes that support our comfortable life: the coal plants, slaughterhouses, smelters, corporate farms, and manifold factories that transform all manner of natural resources into the growing stream of energy, food, and products that we happily consume. We are therefore easily convinced that we are treading lightly upon the earth, that nature is not the source of our food and shelter and tools and VCRs but is rather a place apart, a sacred space of leisure, tranquillity, and purity.

This conception of nature as untouched and pristine has been particularly strong in the US. Gardener Michael Pollan notes that Americans have done fine work in preserving

This conception of nature as untouched and pristine has been particularly strong in the US

places considered wilderness and 'a terrible job of managing the rest of our land,' for once a landscape is no longer 'virgin' it is typically written off as fallen, lost to nature, irredeemable.'[4]

Environmentalism has been more concerned with offering a symbolic escape from modernity than a programme for coming to terms with it. Our approach to animals conjures up a child-like utopia in which wild creatures are both free and friendly, a *Nemo* never-never land where clownfish fathers worry about their sons instead of eating them and no animals are inconvenienced, let alone killed, by human activity. Historian Keith Thomas observes that 'nature parks and conservation areas serve a function not unlike that which toy animals have for children; they are fantasies which enshrine the values by which society as a whole cannot afford to live.'[5] Radical environmentalists are more consistent than mainstream nature lovers inasmuch as they argue that healthy ecosystems demand dramatic reductions in human consumption. But it is sometimes unclear if rejecting the western tradition is the means or the end, and many radicals seem driven by desires that seem more psychological and utopian than practical. Susan Zakin points out that radical environmentalists such as Edward Abbey and Dave Foreman posit and advocate a sort of absolute freedom 'that is possible only in childhood' – or in our memories of childhood.[6]

'Man seeks to draw from nature the meaning he cannot find in society,' explained social critic Leo Lowenthal in 1937. Nature loving offers us the possibility of becoming 'a "thing," like the tree or brook, and find more pleasure in this surrender than in a hopeless struggle against manmade forces.'[7]

This often reflexive hostility towards practical matters helps to explain why widespread nature loving has not translated into stronger environmental laws and policies. Successful political movements require considerable tolerance for friction and frustration, working through differences in philosophy and personality, building coalitions, testifying at public hearings, creating and maintaining bureaucratic institutions to monitor and regulate industry. Determining sustainable levels and patterns of resource use and designing technologies that will enable people to live in an ecologically sustainable manner demands a great deal of scientific research and technological innovation. These are precisely the sort of tedious, quintessentially modern activities that so much of nature loving, from Rousseau to Abbey, has been calculated to escape.

Ever since the Enlightenment we have turned to nature – forests, fields, trees, dogs, dolphins, ecosystems – for meaning

Nature loving has often constituted a distraction from the work of bequeathing a liveable planet to our progeny, has been more about transcending the constraints of life than adapting to them. Ever since the Enlightenment we have turned to nature – forests, fields, trees, dogs, dolphins, ecosystems – for meaning.

Sometimes this search for meaning has led to preserving selected landscapes or species. But pet ownership, backpacking, gardening, exotic vacations, visits to the Nature Company and zoos more often dovetail with the imperatives of industrial capitalism, the increased consumption of nature. Our acts of nature loving have expressed our unease with material comfort while seldom challenging or changing it.

Yet certainly our collective future depends on our ability to make ourselves at home here, to make our peace with and adjust ourselves to the earth's constraints even as we celebrate its beauties.

Notes

1 Scruggs, L. (2003) *Sustaining Abundance: Environmental Performances in Industrial Democracies*. Cambridge, Cambridge University Press, p. 76.

2 Bess, M. (2000) 'Greening the Mainstream: Paradoxes of Antistatism and Anticonsumerism in the French Environmental Movement,' *Environmental History*, 5, pp. 15–16.

3 Davis, S.G. (1997) *Spectacular Nature: Corporate Culture and the Sea World Experience*. Berkeley, CA: University of California Press, p. 242.

4 Pollan, M. (1991) *Second Nature: A Gardener's Education*. New York, NY: Dell, p. 223.

5 Thomas, K. (1983) *Man and the Natural World: A History of the Modern Sensibility*. New York, NY: Pantheon, p. 301.

6 Zakin, S. (1993) *Coyotes and Town Dogs: Earth First! And the Environmental Movement*. New York, NY: Penguin, p. 181.

7 Lowenthal, L. (1978) 'Knut Hamsun,' in A. Arato and E. Gebhardt (eds), *The Essential Frankfurt School Reader*. New York, NY: Urizen Books, pp. 320–1.

References

Animal Wellness Magazine (2003) 5, 4.

Coates, P. (1998) *Nature: Western Attitudes since Ancient Times*. Berkeley, CA: University of California Press.

Findlen, P. (1994) *Possessing Nature: Museums, Collecting, and Scientific Culture in Early Modern Italy*. Berkeley, CA: University of California Press.

Jansen, A., et al. (1998) 'Environmental Challenges and Institutional Changes: An Interpretation of the Development of Environmental Policy in Western Europe,' in K. Hanf and A. Jansen (eds), *Governance and Environment in Western Europe: Politics, Policy and Administration*. Edinburgh Gate: Longman.

Mackenzie, J.M. (1997) 'Empire and the Ecological Apocalypse: The Historiography of the Imperial Environment,' in T. Griffiths and L. Robin (eds), *Ecology and Empires: Environmental History of Settler Societies*. Edinburgh: Keele University Press.

Index